WEIRDVOLUTION

Adventism for a Post-Church Generation

Marcos D. Torres

ISBN: 978-0-6485652-8-4

Self-Published by Marcos D. Torres/ The Story Church Project

For permissions or information contact:
pastormarcos@thestorychurchproject.com

Cover by Ford Filomeno

Image Source: All images in this book come from Canva.com

ACKNOWLEDGEMENTS

I would like to thank my wife, first and foremost, for all of her support and encouragement in life and ministry. And of course, for proofreading this book to make sure it made some kind of sense. You are the best.

To Mike Manea and Adrian Zahid for all of their feedback and insights and to Professors Nicholas Miller and Fernando Canale of Andrews University, for introducing the key foundational concepts that made this project possible. Thank you, guys, for all your work.

Finally, my deepest thanks to God who has led me, journeyed with me and inspired me to know him more and tell the world his story. May I long each day to know you just a little more

CONTENTS

INTRODUCTION: THE ANSWER IS WEIRD

Before you dive into the book I have a confession to make.

I love Adventism.

There. I said it. Glad that's off my chest! I feel a few pounds lighter now.

All jokes aside though, this wasn't always the case. While today, Adventism has given me what I consider to be the most beautiful story of God, some years ago I was ready to leave. Legalism had all but beaten me to the ground. I lived in a perpetual state of anxiety and I was done.

But then, I started to see the light. A little here, a little there. I started to see Jesus emerging throughout our story and then one day, it hit me. Jesus *is* our story.

Once I saw Adventism through Jesus-glasses everything started to change. And the more I saw Adventism in light of his heart, the more amazed I became. Today, I declare in the most politically incorrect way – Adventism is the most beautiful story of God the world has ever known. Jesus is its centre.

Now, you may be wondering what any of this has to do with the title of the book, "Weirdvolution: Adventism for a Post-Church Generation." The answer to that question will unfold as we progress. But here is the bottom line. If you want to reach post-church society then you have to discover, first and foremost, how weird Adventism is.

The reason is simple. Our church and its leaders have been conditioned to believe that transforming our churches is just a matter of methodology. We read all the latest books on church growth and try to apply its principles to our local churches. I tried this. You know what I ended up with? A super well organised group of spiritless and lifeless people who were just as dead as they were before the method was changed. Methodology is not the saviour.

If you are reading this book because you are curious about another method then please, stop. That's not what this book is about at all. In fact, it's about the opposite. True church transformation doesn't come from methods just as a beautiful marriage is not achieved by merely applying marriage expert advice. A marriage thrives when it is fuelled by love. The advice of the experts is helpful only when love is the story that is being told. Get rid of the love but keep the methods, and you end up with a couple who live like civilised roommates. Add love to the mix, and you end up with a contagious passion that completely redefines that couples entire existence.

Church is like that.

A lot of people miss this. They think they will just get the latest book on strategies and methods and boom, they will have a revived church. But it doesn't ever really work. And the reason is they have skipped the most foundational step of them all – our love-story as it is in Jesus.

But once that love-story is introduced and embraced, your church will change. There may not be any methods or strategies just yet. But you will see and experience a shift. So before you go to war with your church members about how they need to change this and that, take them on a love-journey toward God's heart. This alone will redefine their entire existence. Add some methodology to that and you will have a church so on fire you won't know what to do with it.

I mean, think about it. Every challenge you face in your local church boils down to people placing self above mission. That's it. Nothing else is at play.

So then we mission hearted people go in there and try and change things. But no one wants to change the things they love. So they resist. Then what do we do? We nag. We stand at the front and pester people with how we all need to be involved and it's a team effort and Jesus is coming soon and blah, blah, blah (trust me, that is pretty much all they are hearing).

But what if there was a better way? What if you could redesign your local Adventist church without all that mess?

How is this possible, you ask? Well, you have to read the rest of this book for the answer. In it you will find the raw material that I use to fuel everything I do. Ill share some ideas on how you can apply that material next.

How You Can Use this Book

1. First, this book isn't just here to give you more theological mumbo jumbo to argue about. Rather, it exists to take you and your church on a journey of discovery. If you truly want to get the most out of this book then, you can't just read it alone. You have to read it with a group and go through the group questions at the end. If you don't, chances are it will be just another book you read and forget. But if you explore it in community, discussing the questions at the end of each chapter, amazing things will happen.

2. Second, I am not infallible. If you and your team read something that you don't gel with don't get hung up on it. The last thing I want is for people to waste more time arguing about theology. So if you disagree with something, feel free to discuss it and move on. The point of this book is its

overarching message. Don't get stuck in the small details.

3. If your church culture happens to be argumentative, ultra-conservative or bordering on fanatical then don't just give this book to the leaders. They are not emotionally prepared to navigate it in a healthy way and you will end up with more headaches. Instead, read the book yourself and organise a sermon series where you can introduce its overarching message in a way that meets them where they are and leads them toward full discovery. Once the culture has evolved in that direction, you can then introduce them to the book and organise some small groups to go over it. Alternatively, you can put together an afternoon training session that goes over the book contents. The small group is, nevertheless, much better because it has a slow-release impact that lasts longer versus the quick release of an afternoon session that tends to be forgotten within a month.

Finally, as I said above while this book is not about methods or strategies, these do have their place. To meet that need I am currently working on the book "*Story-Church: Awakening Your Church's World Changing Identity.*" To know when it is released and ready for purchase make sure you subscribe to the Newsletter at thestorychurchproject.com. (You get the eBook "*How to Study the Bible with Postmoderns*" for free just for subscribing.)

Are you ready to discover an Adventism for our post-church generation?

I hope so. Things are about to get weird.

CHAPTER 1: ADVENTISM IS *NOT* WEIRD.

A couple of years ago I ran into an article that was summarizing a talk given by an official in the church. Although I have since forgotten where the article was located there is one thing I have not forgotten - the boiling sense of irritation as I read a quote from this official complaining of the rising trend to make Adventism appear like other denominations.

Some reading this book may be thinking just about now, *Hey, I like the fact that this "official" said what he said. I'm not sure I'm going to like this book anymore!*

If that's the case all I can say is this. Stick around. You may just be surprised. This chapter and the next are the launch pad from which the main point of the book emerges in chapter 3. So don't skip out too early.

Now here's the reason why those words vexed me so much. Having grown up a conservative Adventist I had become exposed to the "us VS them" mentality for far too long. In my experience, such a mentality did nothing but breed narcissism, elitism and ignorance. And I was tired. Tired of the ridiculous arrogance that continued to be passed around as "faithfulness" or "love of truth". I am referring to the idea that Adventism is somehow better than other denominations, that we have no need to learn from other Christians, that we should only ever read Ellen White and other conservative Adventists while refusing to read anything written by fellow evangelicals (or more progressive Adventists). I am referring to this rebarbative sectarian attitude that somehow places everyone else in the category of "Babylon" and us in the category of "remnant" with no grey in between. I was done with it.

At that point in my life I had benefited greatly from discovering how Adventism was like other denominations. It was a breath of fresh air. I also enjoyed reading books written by fellow Christians in other denominations. I learned a lot from them and came to appreciate and highly value their faith journey and heritage. I attended their churches and was amazed at how simple and contagious their love for Jesus was. I was motivated by their passion and excellence. But most of all, I had found that my faith heritage was rooted in the same soil as theirs. That I really wasn't that different from them neither practically, historically nor theologically. We were all protestants. We all held to the five solas of the protestant reformation. Martin Luther was as much their hero as he was mine. The dangers of the legalism that had enveloped the medieval church was just as repulsive to them as it was to me. And from John Calvin down to John Wesley there was a continuum of truth that we all shared. I learned Adventism wasn't born in a vacuum but instead derived its identity from the same pool where the "Sunday churches" gleaned theirs. Through the journey of exploring the faith of my fellow Jesus-followers I came to appreciate Adventism more. I had discovered, for the first time, an Adventism divorced of sectarian ideology and self-adulating platitudes. One that had a beauty securely planted in the person of Jesus and did not need, even for a moment, to put another denomination down in order to make up for its own deficiency.

Perhaps now, the reader can better understand why I found the GC officials' statement so vexatious. Grant it, I had no way of knowing exactly what he meant. But that was how I interpreted it based on my own emotionally unstable experience with the church. I wanted Adventism to be the same as others. I hated the way in which we, with our misguided zeal, had taken such a beautiful message and managed to morph it into such a repulsive narrative that the rest of the Christian world found need to label us a cult. For me, this officials' words were a reminder of the very thing I saw as detrimental to our mission and identity.

However, the story doesn't end there.

At the age of 29 I became a local Adventist pastor. I was excited! I felt God call me to ministry at 17 and now, 12 years later, it was finally official. I was ready to change the world.

But then I hit a wall. Everywhere I went and looked, Adventist churches were either dead or dying. A successful local Adventist church was about as mythical as a unicorn. I wasn't totally surprised of course. I grew up in the church. I had seen this for decades. But now I was a leader and it hit me even harder. I wanted to change the world. I wanted to do something meaningful. And the church was just there, taking up space and talent that could be better used elsewhere.

However, I didn't give up. I read the best books, took the neatest methods and strategies and put them to practice. In my mind, so long as we restructured and refocused a few things, the churches would evolve and change. But it didn't work.

At this point, most would give up. But I kept digging. There had to be a core – an epicentre – to this deadwood experience in the local Adventist church and I wanted to know what it was.

One of the methods I had learned from the many books I read was asking people why their church existed.

So I visited. One person. Ten people. Fifty. I've since lost count.

I asked all of them. Why does your church exist? I wanted to know.

In time a pattern started to emerge. And the more I repeated this exercise the more the pattern was confirmed. Regardless of a person's time in church, background, theological bent or culture I discovered they all had one thing in common. When it came to the question "Why does your church exist?" not a single person had anything inspiring to say. Not one.

The pieces of the puzzle started to come together. If no one had anything inspiring to say about their purpose as an Adventist church, then what I was dealing with was groups of people who were both uninspiring and uninspired. And what happens when you give an uninspired church strategies and methods? You get a well-organized uninspiring bunch of people. And that's if they even plug into your strategy – which most of them wont.

I realized that if I was ever going to revive my churches it would take more than some slick method or pathway to discipleship and ministry. If I was ever going to revive my church I needed to go back to the story of Jesus. We all did. We needed to fall in love with why we exist as Adventists once again. While the strategies and plans could serve as the engine to the church, Jesus was the fuel. And we were in need of a refill.

This realization brought me back to the question of Adventism's identity – you know, the one I didn't like. Despite how annoyed I was at people who harped on about the uniqueness of Adventism, I finally realized that maybe that was something I needed to figure out.

So I began a journey of encounter. I wanted to know what makes Adventism relevant (if it even was relevant). Throughout the journey I discovered that every belief system, regardless of its origin and creed, is essentially a story. It has something to say to us about us but also about more than us. It strings together the complexity of reality into a plot line that promises to give us purpose, direction and clarity. This is the nature of every ideology – they are stories at their core.

This realization forced me to ask, *What is Adventism's story? What do we have to say that is worth saying?*

In the pages that follow I will share my journey and offer how the discoveries I made energized my ministry in ways methods and clever plans never could. Through this adventure, I encountered the beauty of Adventism in a way that Sabbath School, Pathfinders and even

Adventist university never gave me. Through this adventure I came to the unavoidable conclusion that there's just something eccentric about what we have to say. We have a perspective to offer the market of ideas – something weird that no one else is saying. We have a Jesus to declare that few have ever heard of, and it's awesome! But before I get to what that is, I want to iron out what our unique message is not.

That's what the next chapter is all about.

Group Questions

1. What has your experience with Adventism been? Positive? Negative? In between?
2. Where are you right now in your relationship to Adventism? Are you frustrated, ready to leave? Are you committed to staying but not sure how to make a difference? Or are you elsewhere?
3. Why does your local church exist?
4. Why are you an Adventist?
5. How do you feel about the idea that Adventism is eccentric? Do you find it offensive? Or perhaps relevant?
6. Do you think knowing our "why" is important toward experiencing revival? Why or why not?

CHAPTER 2: OK. ADVENTISM IS NOT *THAT* WEIRD.

Growing up Adventist many people spoke as if we somehow just dropped out of the sky with all this truth no one had ever heard of before. Nicolas Miller expressed it well when he wrote "Some Adventists appear to believe that our founders sat in a room with their Bibles and put together an entirely new set of beliefs and practices, thus building a New Testament church from scratch"[1]

For some, this mythological view of ourselves makes us special. Everyone else had a few things here and there, but for the most part they were wrong. And we were right. As I mentioned in the previous chapter, this kind of mentality bred a sense of narcissism among us resulting in a self-aggrandizing view that placed us on a higher platform than other protestant and evangelical Christians.

This kind of mentality is also the main thing that keeps us from seeing just how relevant and eccentric we really are. Because when we convert people on the basis of how right we are and how wrong others are, we end up with a culture focused on itself and not Jesus. We end up with propaganda that we label theology, self-praise that we label present-truth and self-promotion that we label evangelism. But when your focus is on telling the story of Jesus, you arrive at this narrative God has graced on us that no one else is telling.

However, before I get to that amazing part of the journey, I want to take this chapter to burst the Adventist bubble by suggesting that, we are not as weird as we like to think we are. Only then will we be ready to appreciate the part of us that is really, truly odd.

Adventist Theology is not that Weird

Like I said at the start, I grew up believing that Adventism was this unique faith tribe that was completely and entirely unheard of. Imagine my surprise when I discovered that nearly all of our beliefs were neatly spelled out and embraced long before we entered the scene.

Yeah, I said it. We aren't that original.

Some of those beliefs came as no surprise to me. I knew other Christians believed in Jesus, the Bible, the second coming etc. I also know we shared beliefs with other Christians like the Trinity, the deity of Jesus, his gospel, church, and eternal kingdom.[2] What I didn't know was how much deeper our similarities went.

For example, Adventists believe that God is love and that as a God of love he has granted free will to all of humanity so that we can choose to love him and serve him in return without being forced to do so. This belief is known as "Arminian theology" which originated with the Deutch reformer Jacobus Arminius (1560-1609) and continues to be the view held by the various Wesleyan and Arminian Baptist denominations.[3] The Arminian approach to scripture is one of those foundational concepts without which Adventism simply would not exist. It is a core teaching and imperative to our identity, and yet, we didn't make it up. It was around centuries before we appeared on the scene.

The Great Controversy motif is also not unique to us. Rather, John Wesley set the foundation for it in what he referred to as scriptures "aesthetic theme". Like Adventists, Wesley had a profound fascination and interest in discovering the truth about the character of God in scripture.

Wesley began his search with the goodness of God and, using his Arminian theology, he discovered that God created all things good and the rebellion of Satan, due to the misuse of his free will, led to the angelic fall and consequently to the fall of man.[4] Like Arminianism, Wesley's aesthetic theme set the foundation and spelled out many of the details Adventists rely on when discussing our Great Controversy narrative.

Adventists also believe that salvation is the free gift of God, not of works which basically every Protestant denomination believes. But we also believe that sanctification is an integral part of salvation, not just justification. The two cannot be separated. One qualifies us for heaven (justification) and the other transforms us into the kind of people who would like to live there forever (sanctification). John and Charles Wesley, the founders of the Wesleyan movement, popularized this unification of justification and sanctification and emphasized

holiness of life more so than their predecessors.[5] This continues to be the view held by
many Methodist, Pentecostal, Nazarene and Wesleyan churches.

In addition, the doctrine of "once-saved-always-saved", which Adventists reject, also has no place in either the Lutheran faith or the Methodist, Pentecostal or Wesleyan traditions. For many years I was led to believe that only Adventists rejected this false belief (which was referred to as "cheap-grace") and thus, we alone had the true gospel. I was shocked when I discovered that all Arminian denominations reject this teaching as well.

So for those of you who like to say that Adventism has some unique take on the gospel... yeah... we don't.

In addition, the teachings that Gods spirit initiates the salvation process in every person to awaken us to our need of him (a reality we cannot awaken ourselves to), that grace can be resisted and the heart hardened against the Holy Spirit and that faith is a gift of God as much as grace were all popularized by Methodism. This means that Adventism's "salvation story" is not actually uniquely Adventist.

What about the doctrine of perfection of Christian character (not to be confused with perfectionism which is totally not cool)? That doctrine also finds its basis in the teachings of Wesley and continues to be held by many who self-identify as Arminian-Wesleyans.[6] Sadly, many Adventists do not realize just how similar our faith is to the Pentecostal traditions rooted in Wesley's thought. Many of us think of Pentecostals simply in relation to their loud worship styles and "speaking in tongues" and fail to realize that we hold much in common with them, and the Wesleyan churches as a whole, when it comes to our understanding of the character of God and the sanctified life.

Likewise, the Adventist view of the Old and New Covenant are identical to the views espoused by the 2nd London Baptist confession (read my other book, "The Hole in Adventism!) held by the Reformed Baptist churches. Both reject infant baptism, teach that NT and OT saints were saved by grace and that the OT nation of Israel typified the church and met its fulfillment in the church. Both also teach that the law is divided into 3 categories (moral, civil and ceremonial) and that the 10 commandments are perpetually binding upon believers even under the New Covenant including the command to honour the Sabbath day and keep it holy.[7]

The doctrine of the Sabbath as a sign between New Covenant believers and God is not unique to Adventism either. The Puritans saw Sabbath observance as an "enduring sign" between God and his people and understood the Sabbath with "covenantal overtones that implied a whole way of life as well as faithfulness to God."[8]

Even the doctrine of the Sabbath as a seal, or test, at the end of time is not unique to Adventism. The Puritan turned Seventh Day Baptist Thomas Tillam saw the Sabbath as a seal at the end of time in contrast to the mark of the beast in Revelation 12 about 200 years before Ellen White, Joseph Bates or Uriah Smith popularized it among the newly formed Advent believers.[9]

In addition we share views with other denominations on baptism by immersion only, the Lords supper as an act of remembrance and spiritual communion with God and church discipline. We also share views on religious liberty, the separation of church and state, creation, the visible return of Jesus and reject a literal and central end-time role for national Israel believing instead that the church is the new Israel.[10]

Even the views we often consider to be unique are not that unique. For example, our belief in the perpetuity of spiritual gifts including the gift of prophecy is shared by many Pentecostal and Wesleyan churches. Our views on the temporality of hell and annihilation of the wicked (over against the eternal torment taught by most protestants) has been gaining acceptance and popularity in evangelical circles for many years now.[11] And our interpretive method for apocalyptic prophecy - historicism - is the historic method used by the reformers when interpreting prophecy. As a result, our views on the antichrist and the papacy did not originate with us.[12]

What about that one doctrine of ours that virtually no one outside of Adventism believes? You know, the 1844 Investigative Judgment thing? Sorry to burst your bubble but it's not that unique either. Adventist scholar Gerhard Phdandl identifies Lutheran Joseph A. Seiss, Catholic author F. Dusterwald and Protestant interpreter T. Robinson among some of the non-Adventists to have arrived at a pre-advent judgment from the book of Daniel.[13] Sure, their views are not identical but the key thoughts are all there.

In addition, the entire doctrine has its roots in Arminian-Wesleyan theology and is impossible to maintain without that foundation. The difference is that for many Arminian-Wesleyans the judgment takes place upon death when the soul goes to heaven. Adventists, on the other hand, believe in soul-sleep which places the judgment at a certain point in human history rather than at each individual death.

In short, while the IJ as a whole may be a uniquely Adventist doctrine it is built on an entirely non-Adventist foundation of Arminian-Wesleyan and soul-sleep theology which was taught by reformers like William Tyndale, many Anabaptists, and surprisingly - Martin Luther himself.[14, 15]

Some would respond by arguing that Adventism's prophetic narrative is definitely unique. After all, we believe that our movement is foretold in prophecy and using the Historicist method, arrive at conclusions in the books of Daniel and Revelation that no one else shares. And this is true. However, we arrive at those conclusions by relying entirely on non-Adventist foundations. We didn't invent Historicism and that's the point. Even the things we proudly think of as "ours" are built entirely on ideas that come from "them".

In fact, even the doctrine of the "remnant church" - intimately connected to the 3 Angles Messages - is beginning to gain acceptance among evangelicals. Current events surrounding the Trump administration and its relationship to American Christianity has caused many to abandon the movement and to begin considering the arrival of a purer faith free of political hunger. Popular evangelical pastor Matt Chandler is among those envisioning a coming persecution fuelled by an apostate Protestantism and aimed at a faithful remnant church.[16]

By the time you get to the end of it it's like, *OK, do we believe anything that's truly original?* The answer is yes, but I will explain that in chapter 3. I will also revisit some of the Adventist beliefs that, while rooted in non-Adventist thought are still fairly unique to us (beliefs like the 3 Angels Messages, Investigative Judgment, End Time Events and Sanctuary which I have touched on above). However, the reality that we must embrace at this juncture is that we are not as unique as we often like to think we are.

How this Affects Mission

The mythical view of our uniqueness is killing Adventism's missional capacity. So long as we, as Adventists, believe that our unique message to the world is something other than Jesus then we will never fulfil our purpose. God did not raise up a movement and bless it like he has this one, just so we can run around telling the world that day seven is the right day to worship instead of day one, that ghosts aren't real or that the Pope is a baddy. He did not pull our pioneers out of the ashes of disappointment so that we could settle on proclaiming that on October 22, 1844 a legal proceeding began in a land far, far away or that if you eat Frichick instead of fried chick you will get an extra ten years to enjoy more Frichick.

Our ideas are not that unique and what we have to say to the world is not that original or relevant. It's just the same old religious drum beating to a different beat. If we want to say anything meaningful to this dying, post-church culture that surrounds us, all that we say must be rooted in, and pointing toward, the person of Jesus. Anything less than this, and we are simply talking to ourselves about ourselves until we are so full of ourselves that we delude one another into believing that we are actually important.

In chapter 3 I will dive more fully into what our unique message is and why it matters so much, but for now I will close this section by summarizing the key points. First, we aren't that original. It's time we lose the big head we have. Second, whatever unique message God has indeed given us must be centred in Jesus or else, what we have to say is of no value at all.

With that said, let's dive into Adventist culture. If our doctrines are not that unique, what about our culture?

Adventist Culture is not that Weird

It's not only our theology that has roots in the broader evangelical tradition. It's our culture as well. "[O]ur founders took many of our beliefs and worship practices from a variety of groups, pressed them through a biblical filter, and adopted and adapted those that remained.... These include midweek prayer meetings, Sabbath school [which we copied from the popular 'Sunday-schools' of the day], camp meetings, the order of the divine service, hymn singing, offering appeals, quarterly Communion services, and many other things."[17]

Interestingly, many Adventist's today act as though learning and applying practices from other denominations is a compromise of our faith. What they fail to realize is that our faith has never had practices uniquely its own. Rather, our pioneers replicated them from the non-Adventist faith traditions from which they came.

In light of all this it is no wonder that Ellen White "joined forces with the Women's Christian Temperance Union, a group of Protestant prohibitionists... [some of whom were pushing for Sunday laws] spoke at their rallies and... recommended that some of our best Adventist talent should work for that organization.... entrusted her signature book, Steps to Christ, to non-Seventh-day Adventists (Dwight Moody's brother) for initial publication [and] thought so highly of non-Adventist theologians and historians that she incorporated their insights—not just their language—into her own books."[18]

Ellen White also "spoke to her largest audiences in non-Adventist settings.... [spoke] in the pulpits of other denominations [and] said some of these contemporary non-Adventist commentaries were among her 'best books.'"[19] Church historian George Knight summarized it well when he wrote,

> It was that same irenic spirit that led Ellen White to suggest that Adventist pastors should become acquainted with other pastors in their district, letting them know that Adventists "are reformers, but not bigots." Her advice was to focus on the "common ground" that Adventism shared with others and 'to present the truth as it is in Jesus' rather than to run down other churches. Using

> such techniques, Adventist pastors could "come near to the ministers of other denominations."[20]

On top of the fact that our culture as Adventists is not unique within the Christian world, it's also not that unique in our world period. Health and plant-based lifestyles are being promoted by atheists and New Age proponents with greater effectiveness than we have had. Our traditional music, dress codes, styles and architecture are borrowed from secular European/ Victorian culture. And our views on the futility of human empire are shared and promoted with greater intensity by social justice proponents in the political sphere.

The grandiose self-centred idea that Adventists are this group of people who emerged from a vacuum and have developed an ideology and practice unheard of in Christian or world history need to be laid to rest. The relevance of Adventism has nothing to do with Adventism and so long as we keep pointing to ourselves and talking about ourselves we will continue to haemorrhage youth and converts by the gallons.

We are not that unique. We are not that weird. We are just another bunch of human beings travelling through life in search of meaning, significance and a hope found only in the person of Jesus. The sooner we recapture that humble, self-abandoning and Christ-centred picture, the sooner we will see an explosion of mission take place in our local churches.

How this Affects Mission

In the next chapter I will explore the contributions and unique elements Adventism brings to the protestant conversation. But for now, we can clearly see that Adventism is not some unheard of faith-tradition with no roots in historic Christian thought. Quite the opposite, our worldview is deeply embedded and indebted to the protestant reformers that came before us. As a result, we have no right to act as if we alone have truth. Rather, we can celebrate our common heritage with our evangelical brothers and sisters. We can worship alongside, pray with and for them, enjoy their biblical resources and learn from their experiences and challenges in the spiritual life.

The idea that Adventism is this uber-unique thing that must not be tainted by contact with a non-Adventist world is one of the myths that kills local church mission. If a pastor gains inspiration by reading a non-Adventist book on church growth and introduces it to the church, some write it off immediately and oppose all of its ideas simply because it isn't Adventist. If an opportunity arises to work with a non-Adventist denomination in some community project, some refuse because they are not Adventist. But apart from these dramatic examples, the very thought process involved in thinking of yourself as better than others kills a person's missional excitement. You simply cannot have a grandiose view of yourself and be a blessing to others in this life. One or the other will win out in the end. And when entire local churches have a grandiose view of themselves, mission always suffers.

The clearest way I have seen this happen is that a grandiose view of oneself always generates a culture of elitism. This in turn paves the way for checklists that we create in our heads. These checklists basically say, "In order for someone to join us they have to be like us. And here are all the boxes they have to tick."

In the end, evangelism may be done in this kind of church but it is a narrow evangelism aimed at reaching only the kind of people who will respond to your checklist. Practically speaking, many of these churches end up geared to reach middle-class people with not too many vices because they are the ones who can most easily tick the boxes of our narrow culture. But the gangsters, prostitutes and misfits can never tick the boxes and even if they try, few are ever able to truly fit in. So in the end, we end up doing evangelism only to those who are most like us and remain incapable of ministering to those who need it the most.

Think about it. What would our churches do if swarms of alcoholics, homeless, druggies and tattoo covered bikkies showed up next weekend. Would we know how to minister to them? What if liberal, left leaning university students decided to attend? Or entire LGBT groups said, "Let's check the Adventist churches out next Saturday." What would our people do? How would they respond?

A grandiose view of ourselves cannot be nurtured alongside an incarnational view of ourselves. We either have our eyes fixed on Jesus and allow him to bring us together with others, or we have our eyes fixed on ourselves and allow the elitism this breeds to isolate us from others. The choice is ours.

Am I Advocating for the "E" word?

At this juncture, some may be concerned that I am advocating for the "E" word. You know what that is. If you ever had an Adventist nightmare, this would be the main villain in there (along with the government outlawing Haystacks). I'm talking about "ecumenism".

So am I advocating for this? My answer is "nah". Ecumenism is totally not my jam. I'll explain more in future chapters. But first, let me offer a bit of nuance when it comes to the "E" word conversation.

In the book Evangelism, Ellen White states that we should not "build up unnecessary barriers between us and other denominations" (573) and to avoid nurturing a "combative spirit" that "closes ears and hearts to the entrance of truth" (574).

These counsels, coupled with her own example explored above, demonstrates that there is a kind of relationship with other denominations that is not problematic or dangerous. Quite the opposite, it is positive and can lead to kingdom growth. The message is therefore clear, as Adventists we are not meant to reject relationships with people of other denominations in the name of doctrinal purity.

Nicholas Miller said it best in his article "Adventism and Ecumenism" when he wrote, "...there is a positive ecumenism and a problematic ecumenism. The positive is about practical, on-the-ground, issue-oriented fellowship, support, and caring between Christians. The negative is a more formal, ideological search for doctrinal and institutional unity."[21]

The evidence demonstrates that Ellen White was in favour of a "positive ecumenism" (to borrow Millers term) and rejected the problematic.

I personally prefer to avoid the term "ecumenism" altogether because of the baggage that it carries. However, I cannot deny that there was a kind of relationship Ellen White envisioned between Adventists and non-Adventists that was mutual and respectful. In other words, she didn't only associate with other Christians to convert them to Adventism and her counsel on inter-denominational relationships, while often evangelistic, is at times simply relational. Ellen clearly exemplified this approach in her own life and counselled our ministers in the same direction.

In fact, one statement that comes as a shock to many is found in Testimonies for the Church Volume 5 pages 583 to 584 where Ellen White states that our ministers could benefit from studying in non-Adventist universities, including theology:

> We would that there were strong young men, rooted and grounded in the faith, who had such a living connection with God that they could, if so counselled by our leading brethren, enter the higher colleges in our land, where they would have a wider field for study and observation. Association with different classes of minds, an acquaintance with the workings and results of popular methods of education, and a knowledge of theology as taught in the leading institutions of

> learning would be of great value to such workers, preparing them to labor for the educated classes and to meet the prevailing errors of our time. Such was the method pursued by the ancient Waldenses; and, if true to God, our youth, like theirs, might do a good work, even while gaining their education, in sowing the seeds of truth in other minds.

Although her counsel is cautious, and in this case purely evangelistic, it nevertheless demonstrates that Ellen White was not advocating a cult-like mentality where Adventists would keep to themselves at all cost. Instead, we see that she was so confident in the truth that she felt those properly grounded in it could study in non-Adventist institutions without fear that they would be led astray and, instead, "do a good work". In her mind, there was something so fundamentally compelling about Adventism's understanding of truth that she had no insecurities about being exposed to other ideological and theological worldviews.

Conclusion

This healthy approach to ideas is something many Adventist churches are missing today and its killing us. The myth that our doctrinal formulation is unique has helped us grow a big head that makes us difficult to approach and also keeps us from recognising just how unconventional and compelling we really are. Because if we really want to know what makes us "peculiar" we have to stop looking at ourselves and look to Jesus.

It is to this unique element of Adventism's narrative that we now turn.

Group Questions

1. Where there any points on theology that surprised you in this chapter? Something you thought was unique to Adventists and found out it isn't?
2. How do you feel about the suggestion that Adventist culture has always borrowed from non-Adventist culture?
3. Do you agree that a grandiose view of ourselves results in practical mission detriment? Or do you disagree?
4. How do you feel about the idea of a positive ecumenism vs a negative one?
5. What changes has this chapter inspired in you? What changes would you like to see in your local church?
6. Change only happens when we put one foot in front of the other and begin the journey. So how will you lead the changes you want to see?

CHAPTER 3: FINE. ADVENTISM *IS* PRETTY WEIRD.

In the previous chapter we identified that hardly anything Adventism believes is uniquely Adventist. So, it's not our "doctrines" that make us weird. Even the ones that we have developed and call our own are built upon foundations that are entirely non-Adventist. We did not just drop out of the sky. We did not re-invent or develop a faith in isolation from all other faith traditions. Rather, we evolved and blossomed from the stories that came before us. When we peel back all the layers of arrogant pride, sectarian ideology and holier-than-thou attitudes we arrive at a faith that is remarkably indebted to historic Christian thought. And yet, there's something eccentric about us. We are protestants yes. But we are also unique.

In order to explain what I mean I need to step out of Adventism a bit and take a brief view at the Christian movement as a whole. We are going to go back in time to the days of burning people at the stake for disagreeing with the Pope and work our way forward through the Protestant Reformation and beyond. By the time you get to the end of this chapter I guarantee this:

your picture of Adventism will be forever changed. You will never be the same and neither will your church. So get ready. Take a deep breath. And here we go!

A Bit of Protestant History

The first inclination of Protestantism is what some refer to as the proto-Protestants (Waldensians, Lollards, and Hussites).[1] These were the movements that protested the wack ideas of the medieval church before the actual Protestant movement began. Then came Luther and, wallah, the Protestant reformation was born.[2]

From the Protestant reformation there emerged two primary camps: the Calvinists, who taught God had predetermined all things including the fall of man, who would be redeemed and, in some circles, who would be lost,[3] and the Arminians who taught God had granted humanity freedom to decide between being saved or lost without him having to "predetermine" their choices.[4]

The Calvinist camp was mainly concerned with the "authority" of God which led it to place great emphasis on his power. It gave birth to denominations like the

Presbyterians, Congregationalists and Episcopalians. The Arminian camp was mostly concerned with the love of God and saw the "dictator God" of Calvinists as antithetical to that love. It gave birth to denominations like the Methodists, Pentecostals and Wesleyans. Adventism, as seen in the previous chapter, emerged mostly from the Arminian camp.

So what is it that makes Adventism unique? The only answer I have ever encountered in my years as an Adventist is that our uniqueness lies in our doctrine of the 1844 pre-advent judgment. However, the idea that "there would be no Seventh-day Adventist Church without the doctrine of the Investigative Judgment"[5] doesn't fully work. While this doctrine certainly plays a role in our uniqueness it ultimately has as its foundation Arminian-Wesleyan soteriology[6] which originated before Adventism was ever thought of. And the peculiar date 1844 doesn't cut it either due to the fact that getting rid of it wouldn't alter Adventist theology in any major way.[7] So if there is something that makes us unique, it's not our doctrine of the judgment.

Allow me to suggest that what makes Adventism unique

is no particular doctrine. Rather, what makes us unique lies in the reason why we embrace the doctrines we do to begin with. Put simply, while all of our doctrines exist outside of our faith in one degree or another, they do so sporadically - here and there and everywhere. However, Adventism is the only movement on the planet in which each of these beliefs come together under a singular narrative. In a sense, that is one of the phenomenon's that makes us unique. But our uniqueness goes deeper. Why is it that Adventist thought has attracted all of these beliefs, almost like a magnet, toward itself? Why are we the only denomination who embraces all of these ideas at the same time?

How Theology Develops

In order to answer this question it is important to understand how theology develops. Contrary to popular belief, theology does not develop by simply reading the Bible. Rather, theology is the result of the following process:

Presupposition

↓

Interpretation

↓

Theology

Here is a simple illustration. Suppose I place a white paper on a table and asked you to look at it. What would you see? The answer is - a white paper. But what if you took a pair of red tinted glasses and put them on? What would you then see? A red tinted paper.

This is exactly how theological reflection works.[8] We all come to the Bible with glasses on and nine times out of ten we don't actually know it. Those glasses have a certain tint to them. That tint is developed by philosophy, culture and various experiences. This is our "presupposition". Over time we become committed to the tint we see (often unconsciously) and we define everything we see according to this tint. This is our "interpretation". So when we come to the Bible we already have these glasses on. When we open to a text that says "the paper is white" our glasses provide us with a tint to interpreting that text as saying "the paper is red". And the result of our presupposition and interpretation is that the "Church of the Red Paper theology" is born.

Here is how it works again:

Presupposition

(Red Glasses)

↓

Interpretation

(Defining what I see by the Red Glasses)

↓

Theology

(The Paper is Red, not White)

This is why saying "Adventism is unique because of 1844" is such an understatement. 1844 is part of our theology. It belongs at the bottom of the process. It is not a presupposition. It is not an interpretive framework. As a result, it and all our other beliefs come in at the end of the theological process, not at the beginning. So the question that will help us identify our weirdness is "what is our presupposition"? In other words, what glasses are we wearing when we come to the text that have led us to embrace the doctrines we hold? The answer to that question reveals what it is that truly makes us unique.

Calvinism, Arminianism and the Big Story

Let's continue our overview of history. Historically speaking, Christians have always viewed Scripture as a story. From beginning to end the Bible, we believe, is telling a grand story that we are invited to know, understand, and enter into. This grand story can be separated into two headings – the Big Story and the Little Story.

The Big Story is defined as the most transcendent part of Scripture's story and deals almost exclusively with who God is and what He is like, apart from creation. The Little Story is related to our local planet. How does the God of the Big Story interact with us in space and time on our local planet? That's the Little Story.

Now that we have ironed that out, let's spend a little while on the Big Story. The most popular understandings of the Big Story within Protestant Christianity are the two groups I mentioned above: Calvinism and Arminianism.

Both of these Big Stories tell different stories of who God is and what he is like.

How exactly does this play out? Let's begin with Calvinism. The Calvinist worldview holds to a particular presupposition. That presupposition is the timelessness of God (Big word I know. Sorry!). Now of course, all Christians believe God exists outside of time. There is no dispute there. But the Calvinist defines timelessness (there it is again) by using a certain philosophical reasoning. This reasoning goes something like this:

> God is Timeless → **Timeless means he cannot experience before and after** (because before and after implies time) → If he cannot experience before and after then he cannot know the future by learning it as that implies before and after → Therefore, God knows the future because he has predetermined it → All of angelic and human history has been predetermined by God's sovereign will including who goes to heaven.

Grant it, this is oversimplified but nevertheless, accurate. And logical as the flow of thought may be, "Arminians [argue] that the Calvinist view owes more to Greek philosophy... than to the Bible's portrait of God."[9] The Bible never defines timelessness so using this speculative definition – which is derived from Parmenides and Plato – as the key to interpreting the Bible is allowing human reasoning to colour the text.[10] And that's not cool.

So here is how the Calvinist system breaks down:

Presupposition
(God's Timeless Nature)
↓
Interpretation
(God has predetermined history)
↓
Theology
(Salvation is only for the few God has predetermined)[11]

The Arminians on the other hand disagree with this worldview. These "concepts", they argue, force a dictatorial and disturbing picture of a God who is anything but love. Thus, Arminianism responds to Calvinism by focusing on the love of God and consequently introduces free-will. This is done in order to preserve the loving nature of God.

Presupposition

(God's Loving Nature)

↓

Interpretation

(Love demands freedom of will)

↓

Theology

(Salvation is for all mankind)

When John Wesley entered the picture, he took Arminianism to the next level. He was concerned with the character of God and began to extrapolate this battle between good and evil in the Bible in order to better understand who God is in light of his love. Wesley, like most other Arminians, found Calvinism disturbing and "felt that the idea of absolute unconditional predestination by divine decree was inconsistent with God's justice, as well as his love and goodness."[12] For Arminians, therefore, the reformation is about returning to the God of love of scripture which Calvinism failed to do.

The Little Story

Now that we have introduced the Big Stories of the Protestant faith let's turn our focus over to the Little Story. In the Little Story the question of how this God from the Big Story relates to, interacts with, and operates with His creation is answered. While the Big Story focuses on who God is and what he is like, the Little Story focuses on planet earth. In theology this encompasses creation, the fall, the flood, the nation of Israel, the church, end time events and the covenants God makes with man.

For Calvinists this Little Story is understood through the "glasses" of God's power. For Arminians, its best understood through the "glasses" of his love. Calvinism developed systematic ways of approaching the Big and Little story known as Covenantalism (Don't worry about how boring that word is. It's not important. Just know that Calvinism has a whole Bible approach that they summarize with a big word and you are good!)[13] This systematic is best understood as a "whole story" approach to the Bible in that it seeks to make sense of all of scriptures themes - from Genesis to Revelation -

through the Calvinist glasses.

However, before we discuss Arminianism's "whole Bible" approach, we need to highlight another contribution it brings to the table. While we have thus far explored the Big Story and the Little Story, Arminianism introduced another element to help make sense of the Bibles narrative and the uniqueness of Adventism. I call it the "Middle Story".

The Middle Story

Put simply, the Middle Story is the story that lies between the Big and Little Story. This "Middle Story" was developed and expounded upon by reformers such as Hugo Grotius, Albert Barnes and, most effectively, John Wesley in what he referred to as scriptures "aesthetic theme".[14, 15] According to Wesley, God was not responsible for evil. Using his love-of-God glasses, Wesley revisited scripture to discover what the origin of evil entailed and there he found a war between good and evil that originated with Satan who used his free will to rebel against God and consequently led humanity into rebellion. So while the Big Story reveals who God is and what he is like, the Middle Story explains how sin originated in light of God's "goodness".

But why exactly is this important? The answer is simple. Calvinists don't need a Middle Story that explains the presence of sin and evil because their "glasses" are deterministic (everything that happens in creation has been predetermined by God). So at the end of the day, there is no need to explain the battle between good and evil.

For Arminians, the most important attribute of God is the attribute of love. Everything is an outflow of God's love, including His power. Therefore, all of God's creation was designed to operate under the law of love – a law which harmonizes only with freedom, because love cannot be coerced, manipulated, or determined. This other-centred paradigm was to be the basis for temporal reality and eternity. However, the concept of God as love is challenged by the presence of evil. How could a loving God allow such things? Such questions lead men to doubt the Big Story and demand an explanation. That explanation is found in the Middle Story.

The Failure of the Arminian Movement

However, as concerned as Arminianism was with the love, justice and character of God and his government the movement failed in one key area: Unlike the Calvinists who managed to interpret the entire Bible through the Calvinist lens and develop a cohesive "whole-Bible" story based on their worldview (that big word we saw earlier), the Arminians never did. As Joseph Dongell pointed out,

> [T]here really is no such thing as Arminian theology, if by that we mean an entire system of thought. Arminian theology, more properly and narrowly defined, pertains only to how one interprets the Bible's teaching about predestination.[16]

While there do exist Arminian approaches that are "whole-Bible" stories based on the Arminian worldview, they are here there and everywhere.[17] In fact, in 2015 *Society of Evangelical Arminians* contributor Brian Abasciano noted that "there are not a lot of good options for a contemporary comprehensive Arminian systematic theology text."[18] DIS

In other words, there is not one central system of thought that brought Arminians together to proclaim their theology of God's love to the world. Instead, Arminianism became more of an approach to understanding God as it relates to individual salvation. Some Arminian groups highlight justification and assurance of salvation (Arminian Baptists, Methodists) while others emphasize holiness and the Holy Spirit (the Pentecostal, Nazarene and Wesleyan holiness/ charismatic movements).[19]

Therefore, apart from a few key thinkers here and there, Arminianism never applied its biblical "love-of-God" presupposition to the entirety of scripture. As a result, they never developed cohesive views that enabled them to approach every theme of scripture - including the law of God, the nation of Israel, the covenants, the church, prophecy, end time events and final judgment from this love-of-God worldview. Thus, in his article "Why I am Not an Arminian" Tim Challies - former Arminian turned Calvinist - wrote,

> Reformed theology (Calvinism) depends not only on key verses but on the warp and woof of the entire Bible. It offers a far more compelling explanation of Scripture than Arminianism, both in its broad outlines and in its fine details.[20]

This absence of a "whole Bible" approach meant that the same movement that began by passionately seeking to redeem the character of God from what they felt was the foul picture of the Calvinist worldview never developed a system of thought that could interpret the entire Bible from that view. As a result, this God-is-love movement never advanced cohesive answers to questions related to the covenants, the law of God, the prophetic timeline, end time events, the Israel/ church relationship, or the judgment of the wicked.

Consequently, the movement splintered with some tending to either adopt already accepted views in those areas, others refusing to answer certain questions and many more caught in endless nuances in-between.

For example, while Arminians rejected the deterministic Calvinist conclusions (God pre-determines everything that happens) they never rejected the timeless view of God which led to that conclusion. This resulted in a system of thought that was internally incoherent. In addition, while Arminians rejected some of the philosophical speculations that Calvinism embraced, they never identified the philosophical speculations they themselves continued to adhere to such as Platonic dualism which gave entry to the doctrine of the immortal soul in Christianity.[21] As a result, to this day Arminianism continues to embrace the self-contradictory view that God is love and has granted freedom of will to his creatures yet torments sinners in hell for all eternity simply because they rejected Christ by exercising the free will he so lovingly gave them. Likewise, how God performs his judgment over humanity was left as a blank area with no real answer - an odd posture for a movement that claimed to defend the justice of God's moral government and his dealings with men.

Enter Adventism

Like the Arminian-Wesleyan world, it was this concern and passion for a renewed understanding of the heart of God and His government that gave birth, though the study of scripture, to the "Great Controversy" theme – Adventism's Middle Story. This theme not only answers questions related to the origin of sin and suffering in the universe but also vindicates God's character from the charges made against him by Satan. And it is in this theme – which emphasizes the loving character of God over and against the presence of evil and suffering – that Adventist theology finds its heart beat. Adventism took these "love-of-God" glasses and embarked on a journey of rediscovering the love of God in every single theme of scripture.[22]

But how? How did Adventism do that which the rest of the Arminian world had not successfully done? While tracing
the history of this is out of the scope of this book, the key that made the difference was the sanctuary.

The sanctuary? You mean that boring doctrine with all the charts and furniture and stuff?

Sort of. Just keep reading.

In the sanctuary the early Adventists discovered the key to applying the love-of-God theme to the entirety of scripture, not just the parts associated with individual justification or holiness. In addition, the sanctuary was foundational in moving Adventist thought from the "timeless God" concept present in both Calvinism and Arminianism to a "God-in-time" view that radically impacted the way in which Adventists think of and relate to God and his relationship with man.[23] As a result Adventism began to revolve around one central theme in scripture: God's desire to be with people - which is the essence of the sanctuary.

Seventh-day Adventist co-founder Ellen White wrote,

> The sanctuary in heaven is the very center of Christ's work in behalf of men. It concerns every soul living upon the earth. It opens to view the plan of redemption, bringing us down to the very close of time, and revealing the triumphant issue of the contest between righteousness and sin.[24]

This statement alone reveals the depth of Adventist thought in relation to the sanctuary. God's love and desire to be with people was their presupposition. Through the sanctuary they discovered the "plan of redemption" from before the foundation of the world to the "very close of time". The focus of this story, however, was not man's salvation but the glory of God. The sanctuary unveiled the battle between good and evil (Middle story) and God's eventual triumph over sin - not though coercion or sheer power, but through the "revelation of his character of love."[25] Thus Ellen White could also write,

> The subject of the sanctuary... opened to view a complete system of truth, connected and harmonious...[26]

For Adventism, the sanctuary reveals the love of God in a way that transcends our own local world and forms a part, in some mysterious way, of the heavenly realm. A sanctuary, which can be best defined as "God's meeting place with man" because he wants to "dwell among them" (Exodus 25:8) in heaven meant that before the foundation of the world the plan of redemption (which is revealed in the sanctuary) was made and through it God has communicated his eternal desire to dwell with us. For

Adventists, this means that his love and grace did not just appear in our space-time realm at the cross. They have been with us all along and continue with us even now. And it is only through this eternal ever-present love that scripture can be properly understood.[27]

In other words, the sanctuary became to Adventists the key by which the Arminian worldview could finally be harmonized into one "whole story" approach to scripture that connected all of its parts in a page by page revelation of the matchless love of God. And it is this single phenomenon that makes Adventism unique.

Thus creation takes on a whole new meaning. It is an act of space-time love. Even the very creation of time itself is an act of love, an idea foreign to the classical theism that under-girds Calvinist thought and continued to impact Arminian thought. Time, to Adventists, was created by God in a specific way - to facilitate both our development and relationship with him.

Under this view, the Sabbath becomes more than a mere moral command. It is the day where God's love and our temporal realm collide in a special way.

The law of God, in this view, is a reflection of his character of love. It is not arbitrary, but the love-parameters upon which life was designed in order for love to flourish. It cannot be abolished as though it was somehow problematic. Rather, he writes it in our hearts under the New Covenant as part of the process of restoring us to the image of love in which he created us.

The covenants, the history of Israel and the church, the gospel, the gifts of the spirit including the gift of prophecy, the health message, the 1260/ 2300 days of Daniel, the pre-advent judgment, the three angels messages, the mark of the beast, the call to come out of Babylon, the remnant church, the second coming, the millennium, the great white throne judgment, the New Jerusalem, the annihilation of the wicked - all of it forms part of this "whole-Bible" story that reveals the unutterable love of God. Thus, the gospel for Adventists doesn't begin in Bethlehem. It begins in Eden and it flows through history into the final consummation of all things.

While many appeal to the cross as the central place where the love of God is revealed, Adventists appeal to all of scripture. All of it is "God with us". It affirms his eternal love in every theme - including Daniel and Revelation. And of course, the Adventist view of non-eternal hell and complete eradication of sin is yet another outflow of this sanctuary God-is-love narrative.

The Investigative Judgement, which has been the subject of much criticism and debate, is all about one thing: God's transparency. God doesn't judge based on his own "all-knowing-ness". Rather, he judges out of love. His judgment is crystal clear. All can observe his decisions. All can see that God is fair and just and loving.

This doctrine, in turn, answers questions about God's judgment and the fairness of his government that other Arminian movements failed to answer.[28] And unlike those who have abandoned Historicism (the historical Protestant method of interpreting prophecy), Adventists have hung on. Because God longs to dwell with us and is always intimately involved with humanity in time, Preterism and Futurism are out. There is just no way that God would leave his people in the dark for that long. Historicism embraces a view of God as present and active in the entirety of human history. Preterism and

Futurism unwittingly deny that by positing most of the prophetic timeline to either the distant past or the distant future.[29]

Time and space do not permit a continued analysis of this. However, for Adventists one thing is clear: God is love – not only in Calvary but in every part of scripture. Thus, Adventism did what the Arminian world never did. It defined the entirety of scripture from the love of God into one cohesive system of thought and then took that story to the world with missions, schools, hospitals, medical and literature ministries, churches, humanitarian aid, publishing houses and more. This is the reason why Adventism has a worldwide ecclesiological system. A congregational system means we can only tell our story sporadically without harmony of thought. A worldwide system means we can tell our story, in a harmonious way, to the entire globe. This is also the reason why the concept of "remnant church" is so central to Adventist thought. It encapsulates the uniqueness of Adventism's narrative in the Christian world.[30]

At the heart of all of this, we find the person of Jesus. He is the sanctuary embodied (Emmanuel – God with us), he is the Lord of the Sabbath, our true rest, the door to heaven, the great high priest, the lamb and the advocate, the resurrection and the life. He is the second Adam, the truth and the way to the fathers heart. If you have seen him, you have seen the father. The Spirit of prophecy the testimony of Jesus and our favourite book as Adventists begins with these words, "A revelation of Jesus..." (Revelation 1:1).

The love of God is our theme. The person of Jesus is our instrument. In him we find all of our meaning and purpose. In Jesus the mission of Adventism – to reveal the truth of God's character to the world – is fulfilled. Jesus is not just part of our message. He is our message through and through.

In Jesus we find a healer. His desire to restore humanity is the only thing that gives meaning to our health message. In Jesus we find the alpha and the omega. His eternal presence is the only thing that gives meaning to our prophetic message. In Jesus we find the true Christ. And without the true Christ, the anti-Christ is a useless topic. All the fame the anti-Christ has it only has because there is a true Christ that the world is hungering for. In

Jesus we find our story, and our significance as the remnant church is lost without the personhood of Jesus and the love of God he came to reveal.

Of course, none if this means that Adventist theology is perfect. We have not discovered everything the Bible has to say on the love of God. We still have questions we can't answer and concepts we find difficult to explain. We continue to grow and learn not only from scripture but from our brothers and sisters in different Protestant traditions. And our picture of God's love and the Great Controversy continues to expand and evolve.[31] But this is OK for Adventists. Our sanctuary view of God sets the foundation for the Adventist concept of "present truth" which means that God is always revealing more truth as time goes by. Thus Ellen White could say,

> Much has been lost because our ministers and people have concluded that we have had all the truth essential for us as a people; but such a conclusion is erroneous and in harmony with the deceptions of Satan, for truth will be constantly unfolding.[32]

For this reason, Adventists have refused to embrace "creeds". Philosophically speaking, a creed is only compatible with a timeless God who is not progressively revealing more truth as human time advances. But a God who willingly enters into time in order to have relationship with us will continue to reveal himself until the end of time. Thus, everything that makes Adventism unique can be traced back to this sanctuary picture of an intimate and loving God who reveals himself to us always within the framework of his love. And while other Protestant traditions may embrace and proclaim the love of God with great passion, Adventism has more than just proclamations about the love of God: it has a robust story that reveals his love in every theme of scripture - Big, Middle and Little Story.

As a result, Adventism has, almost like a magnet, attracted all doctrines to itself that celebrate the love of God and in turn built on them and discovered truths for this day that had not been discovered before. This sanctuary God who dwells among us, interacts with us and condescends to us in every step of the story is the God we find, not only in the cross, but all throughout scripture. In every theme, teaching and mystery -

including the law, judgment, prophecy and the war between good and evil - there Adventism sees a beautiful being, with a character of love unlike anything man could ever imagine.

Revisiting Some of those Key Adventist Doctrines

In the last chapter, I promised I would touch again on some of Adventism's most unique doctrinal ideas like the 3 Angels Messages, Investigative Judgment and our Prophetic Narrative. I mentioned how each of these is ultimately rooted in non-Adventist thought but some of you may have felt unsatisfied by my explanation since, it remains true that to some degree we are indeed the only ones who believe those frameworks in the way in which we express them. At this point, I am now ready to make my final observation on these more unique aspects of our theology by making one simple observation. If you look at the most unique elements Adventism brings to the table, (such as those doctrines described above) all of them are story lines. Unlike specific doctrines like Sabbath, death or hell (doctrines we share with many other Christians) the doctrines most uniquely ours are not "specific" or "point" doctrines but rather "narratives". The 3 Angels Messages is a phrase that refers not only to Revelation 12 but to the entirety of Adventist theology and the war between good and evil. The Investigative Judgement is a theme that develops out of the Great Controversy and flows out of a judgment process that includes Jesus historic death, a present end-time judgment and the final Great White throne judgment at the end of time. Our prophetic narrative takes into account the flow of human history. Virtually every unique idea Adventism brings to the table is not a "point" doctrine but rather a "narrative" that takes into account past, present and future – just like the Sanctuary.

So yes, Adventism does have an eccentric theological narrative. But that alone does not make it unique. Rather its presuppositions derived from Sola Scriptura set the foundation that enables the denomination to embrace the narrative it has. Here is our system using the above process.

Presupposition

(The Sanctuary - God is love/in time)[33]

↓

Interpretation

(God's love is the interpretive lens for all of scripture)

↓

Theology

(Gods law, gospel, prophecies etc. all reveal his love)

Perhaps no one has summarized the purpose and mission of Adventism as well as Ellen White did when she wrote,

> It is the darkness of misapprehension of God that is enshrouding the world. Men are losing their knowledge of His character. It has been misunderstood and misinterpreted. At this time a message from God is to be proclaimed, a message illuminating in its influence and saving in its power. His character is to be made known. Into the darkness of the world is to be shed the light of His glory, the light of His goodness, mercy, and truth. The last rays of merciful light, the last message of mercy to be given to the world, is a revelation of His character of love.[34]

Conclusion

Without Adventism the Christian world would have two narratives to offer. A scary but whole Bible approach known as Calvinism. Or a loving but surface approach known as Arminianism. However, in Adventism we discover the first and only love-of-God whole Bible approach in existence. There simply is no other.

And this is why your church exists.

It exists to communicate the only whole Bible approach to the love of God this world has ever known. It exists to proclaim Jesus with a clarity and beauty human ears have never heard.

Adventists. We are it. If we don't do this, no one will.

And yet, there remains one glaring question. If these things are true, why is Adventism so "non-loving" to so many people? Why have our preachers tended to emphasize a scary picture of judgment, perfectionistic ideologies and - quite frankly - legalistic and man-centred theology? Why are so many of our churches cold and dead? The answer to that question will come in the next chapter.

Until then let's celebrate Adventism.

Group Questions

1. How do you feel when you read that Adventism is the only whole Bible approach to the love of God in the world? Does this redefine how important our message is?
2. The chapter ends with these words, "Adventists. We are it. If we don't do this, no one will." How do those words make you feel?
3. Do you finally understand why Adventism matters and what makes it unique? If so, share your reaction to this with your group.
4. Adventism finds its meaning only in Jesus. How often is Jesus proclaimed in your church? How passionately is he pursued?
5. What changes can you bring to your church to begin turning its focus toward Jesus and away from other things?

CHAPTER 4: BUT, WE AREN'T WEIRD-WEIRD ARE WE?

By now you have seen that Adventism is both completely rooted in historic Protestant thought while simultaneously adopting a whole new way of viewing the story of scripture. This new way has resulted in the most complete Biblical approach to the love of God which impacts how we interpret every other theme of scripture. The end result is a theology that is focused on Jesus and revealing God's character of love in a way not found in any other denomination.

And that makes us weird. But the next question we need to explore is, does that make us weird-weird? As in, the kind of weird that is you know... awkward?

This is a good question because it's one thing to have a unique narrative and it's a whole other thing to be just plain cultish, and repulsively bizarre. But isn't that what Adventism is like to many people? If so, why? If we have this unique and wholistic approach to the love of God, then why is Adventism so "non-loving" to so many people? Why have our preachers tended to emphasize a scary picture of judgment, perfectionism and legalistic/

man-centred theology? Why have we promoted doom and gloom pictures of the end times that sound more like conspiracy ramblings than a revelation of the love of God? Why are so many of our churches cold and dead?

In order to give a satisfactory answer to these questions, we need to take a brief trip through the history of Adventist culture. Before I begin I do need to note that this is not going to be a detailed or exhaustive study on SDA history. Plenty of resources exist that do that well. In this chapter, I want to keep things as simple as possible without being shallow. By the end, I hope to show that while Adventism is weird, it's definitely not weird-weird. Let's get started.

A Bit of SDA History

When Adventism was born, a large portion of North Americans were already Christians. The Second Great Awakening, which resulted in lots of conversions, was just beginning to wind down.[1] As a result, Adventist preachers glossed over the stuff everyone already knew (like the gospel) and placed a heavy focus on the more eccentric teachings of the church. Among these teachings was the Adventist emphasis on the Sabbath. Although Adventism shared a view of the law identical to other churches[2] there remained disagreement over whether the Sabbath command applied to the first-day or the seventh-day of the week. In addition, a new way of interpreting the Bible began to gain popularity about the 1870's[3] and taught that "Christians are not under the law in any sense".[4] Adventists, of course, saw this as a dangerous teaching and reacted to it (perhaps a bit too much).[5] To make matters more interesting, certain laws requiring the observance of Sunday as a day of rest were being enforced by local governments.[6]

Due to this context, Adventist preachers and evangelists came to focus almost exclusively on themes like the law and its relation to end time events. The unfortunate result was that emerging generations of Adventists were raised on a "law diet" and heard very little of the gospel.[6] Over time the church came to lose sight of the gospel completely. Ellen White herself noted that during these years "many had lost sight of Jesus".[7] Adrian Zahid captured this well when he wrote,

> Sermons that once were preached with vigor and the freshness of a new discovery had, by the 1880's, grown, as Ellen White put it, as "dry as the hills of Gilboa." The emphasis had shifted from what Christ was doing for us to what we could 'do' for Him. In other words, the message of righteousness by faith had become righteousness by the law.[8]

In 1888 the message of grace was re-introduced to Adventists by two preachers named E.J. Waggoner and A.T. Jones in what would become the most historic conference in SDA history - the 1888 General Conference. The conversation turned explosive when Waggoner disagreed with the traditional Adventist interpretation of the law in Galatians being the ceremonial law. According to Waggoner, Galatians was talking about the Ten Commandments, not just the ceremonial law. This view introduced a huge shift for the church which "[f]or three decades... had interpreted that law as the ceremonial law."[9] According to Adventist leaders, that belief was key in protecting the view that the law had not been done away with.

As a result, Jones and Waggoner stood against the legalism that had taken hold of the church. But it wasn't overt legalism that Jones and Waggoner were confronting. Adventists still had enough tradition in them to avoid believing that a person could be saved by works. Instead, Adventists tended to emphasize law so much that grace, while never denied, became a non-essential point.[10] When Jones and Waggoner entered the scene they preached Christ as the only hope, de-emphasized the law and, instead, lifted up Jesus. Ellen White stood by their side and expressed her support in statements such as:

> You will meet with those who will say, 'You are too much excited over the matter. You are too much in earnest. You should not be reaching for the righteousness of Christ, and making so much of that. You should preach the law.' As a people we have preached the law until we are as dry as the hills of Gilboa, that had neither dew nor rain. We must preach Christ in the law, and there will be sap and nourishment in the preaching that will be as food to the famishing flock of God. We must

> not trust in our own merits at all, but in the merits of Jesus of Nazareth.[11]

And,

> Some of our brethren are not receiving the message of God upon this subject. They appear to be anxious that none of our ministers shall depart from their former manner of teaching the good old doctrines. We inquire, Is it not time that fresh light should come to the people of God, to awaken them to greater earnestness and zeal? The exceeding great and precious promises given us in the Holy Scriptures have been lost sight of to a great extent, just as the enemy of all righteousness designed that they should be. He has cast his own dark shadow between us and our God, that we may not see the true character of God.[12]

Many Adventists at the time, unaccustomed to a Christ centred approach to their worldview, interpreted the preaching of Jones and Waggoner as dangerous and feared that, if fully embraced, it would destroy

Adventism. They even rejected Ellen White's support of Jones and Waggoner with some claiming she had, in her old age, been led astray by the young preachers. To make matters worse, the General Conference president of the day along with one of the church's top theologians, fought vehemently against Jones and Waggoner and "held that the new interpretation undermined Adventism's traditional position on the end-time importance of the law of God."[13]

At this point, we can begin to see signs that the "God-is-love/ with-us" glasses that Adventism was based on had been replaced with "law-glasses" instead. Such a system of thought is bound to lead to the legal and Christ-less religion that Ellen White reacted against. Thus, "[i]n contrast to Ellen White, many of the leading brethren who heard the sermons delivered by Waggoner and Jones in Minneapolis were irritated by them."[14]

Following the controversial conference, Ellen White dedicated more time to emphasizing Jesus as "our only hope for time and eternity"[15] and many in the church began to see the light. However, it was clear that two diverse Adventism's were now emerging. One saw Jesus and his work in the sanctuary as central in the entire narrative of salvation. The other saw the same story primarily through the lens of the law. Thus Ellen White could say,

> The Lord has sent a message to arouse His people to repent, and do their first works; but how has His message been received? While some have heeded it, others have cast contempt and reproach on the message and the messenger. Spirituality deadened, humility and childlike simplicity gone, a mechanical, formal profession of faith has taken the place of love and devotion. Is this mournful condition of things to continue? Is the lamp of God's love to go out in darkness?[16]

Fast forward over 60 years and Adventism had undergone some pretty major changes including the death of Ellen White in 1915 and the arrival of a new and rigid method of relating to the Bible known as "fundamentalism".[17, 18] The remaining law-culture, combined with the rigidity of fundamentalism, proved to have a "bewitching" influence. The combination gave birth to an era marked by a "legalistic style of argumentation and behavior"[19] that fed the flames of narcissism, sectarian ideology and irrational applications of lifestyle standards that proved impossible to defend from scripture as new generations emerged to question the status quo.[20]

During this time myths regarding the ministry, application and proper use of late church prophetess Ellen White, among other exaggerations of Adventist thought, developed.[21] This all set the ground work for the next explosion in the 1950's when a series of discussions began between Adventist leaders and Calvinist-Evangelicals who wanted to know, from the horse's mouth, what Adventists really believed. The discussion was published in a book known as *Questions on Doctrine* (*QOD*).

After the book's publication, the two Adventism's collided once more. Some claimed the book was a proper reflection of Adventist thought. Others considered it a departure from Adventist thought. Among those who opposed it was conservative theologian M.L. Andreasen. Andreasen felt that the authors of *QOD* had misrepresented Adventism in their dialogues with the

Calvinists and expressed his concerns to them, but the conversations did not go well. As a result, Andreasen took it upon himself to expose the church leaders and accused them of changing SDA theology in order to pacify the Calvinists. The result was an all-out war. And it was through the attention that came through the controversy that Andreasen came to promote what became one of the most popular narratives in Adventist thought: *Last Generation Theology* (LGT).[22]

While LGT held a lot in common with classic Adventist thought, it's greatest departure was that it interpreted the Adventist narrative through the glasses of "perfectionism" instead of the sanctuary. This resulted in morphing Adventist theology into a man-centred story which held that in order for Jesus to return Adventists had to first overcome all of their sins and reach a point of sinless perfection where they would no longer need a mediator to intercede for them. Proponents of this view also obsessed over themes such as the human nature of Christ, strict standards of Sabbath keeping, vegetarianism, dress reform, end time events and the need for complete sinless perfection.[23] In short, they replaced the Adventist sanctuary-glasses with a fanatical version of Wesleyan-Holiness theology and reinterpreted Adventism through it. The result saw many Adventists returning to a Pharisaic mode of relating to the Bible.

For example, Adventist youth raised under this way of thinking will often relate how they were taught it was a sin to go beyond the knees into a beach/ lake on Sabbath. So long as the water stayed under the knees they were not sinning. If it went over they were guilty of "breaking the Sabbath". Regardless of how ridiculous this sounds today, the teaching appealed to the spirit of Adventism which, in 1888, had sided with a law-centred vision.

The SDA church never accepted LGT in any official capacity, however, LGT became the glasses through which the majority of conservative Adventists read the Bible.[24] Those who shared in the spirit of the men and women who argued that an emphasis on Jesus in 1888 would lead Adventism astray, who pushed for the adoption of fundamentalism into the Adventist framework, and who, in the 1950's sided with Andreasen in attacking SDA leadership and accusing it of apostasy, went on to promote the LGT brand as the only true version of Adventism. However, many others rejected these developments. Thus, the undercurrent of division from 1888 manifested itself with greater force. Many followed Andreasen as though his teachings represented the true, historic theology of the pioneers and came to view themselves as "Historic Adventists" while others rejected his teachings. To this day, one could say that the mainstream SDA church is primarily split into two camps: 1) the Andreasen's and 2) everybody else.

New generations were now raised with a similar narrative as the pre-1888 Adventists - one that emphasized the law, judgment and apocalyptic themes to such a degree that Jesus - while never denied - was minimized. The new mantra of the Adventist voice was perfection, perfection, perfection or Christ will not come. Legalism spread. Lack of assurance of salvation dominated the lives of the members. A fanatical approach to the health message and end time events demoralized the pulpits and churches. Independent ministries promoting Andreasen's theology published magazines, hosted programs and offered resources that continued to feed the legalism and spread distrust of church leadership. Thus, the stage was set for the next great divide in the Adventist church – the Desmond Ford crisis. Adrian Zahid summarized it best when he wrote,

> Decades of teaching members to 'prepare' for the Judgment had led many to develop an unhealthy fear of it. Dr. Desmond Ford, a preeminent Australian theologian, brought to the attention of the Church his rejection of the Sanctuary doctrine as a foundational "pillar" of Adventism. He replaced it instead with the soteriological vision of Protestant theology. Depicting his own perspective as a solution to the 'fear' that people felt regarding the Judgment, he emphasized the 'assurance' we could have by knowing the essence of the Gospel.[25]

Although other Adventist theologians at the time were coming to terms with the gospel and rejecting the influence of LGT and its perfectionistic glasses, Ford pushed ahead with the belief that the problem with Adventism had to do with the sanctuary doctrine itself. However, it was never the sanctuary doctrine that was problematic but the way in which it had been reinterpreted through perfectionist ideology. And it was this foundation of legalism and fundamentalism that created the context for Ford to have the impact he did. Thus, Mike Manea could say that "had it not been for Andreasen's heretical influence, it is highly unlikely that Ford's apostasy would have resonated with anyone else in the church".[26]

Again, Ford's solution to the tortured consciences of Adventists everywhere was to emphasize the assurance of salvation and reject the sanctuary doctrine which he saw as an assurance killer.[27] The church was rocked to its core. Many members and pastors abandoned ship. Critics pummelled it from the outside with questions that demanded answers. The Adventist mythology, born out of the unholy union of legalism and fundamentalism finally came crumbling down.

In reaction to the decades of legalism and the influence of Ford, a new Adventism began to emerge to counter the law-culture. Thankfully, this new Adventism was not afraid to admit its limitations. It was not afraid to wrestle with the difficult questions and to uplift Christ no matter the cost. Through the influence of this new Adventism, the era of legalism and fundamentalism began to meet its end. However, there was one fatal flaw. This new Adventism, wonderful as it was, was too reactionary to the Historic camp. Rather than restoring the sanctuary-glasses that led Adventism to a whole-Bible view of God's love this reactionary movement made the assurance of salvation its new set of glasses. Consequently, it emphasized 1888 and the gospel but downplayed, and at times rejected, foundational aspects of Adventism's classical narrative.

The results appeared to be two fold. On the one hand, former Adventists returned to the church and a new generation was raised with Christ as the centre of their worldview. On the other hand, those who dug deep enough discovered that they had little in common with classical Adventism. Many found themselves unable to reconcile their grace-centred theological lens with some of Adventism's core beliefs which they still saw through the lens of perfectionism. In the end, many mistakenly concluded that Adventism simply wasn't compatible with the gospel. As a result, studies began to "[indicate] that more and more church members [were] leaving because they... changed their beliefs".[28] Others disconnected from the unique teachings or attempted to undermine them from the inside. But the most common trend was simply to minimize their relevance. Thus, two major studies conducted by the church identified that among Adventist youth in North America, core Adventist teachings such as the sanctuary and the remnant church found less acceptance than widely accepted teachings like the gospel, creation and the Sabbath.[29] In short, while this new reactionary Adventism had succeeded in restoring a gospel/ Jesus-centred vision to Adventism it has underplayed, misunderstood and, at times, opposed its whole Bible approach to the love of God.

Here is a brief overview of what we have explored:

> **Classical Adventism:** Began with a "God is love/ with us (sanctuary)" presupposition that was used to interpret the entire Bible to arrive at a complete system of truth that celebrated the centrality of Jesus and the beauty of God's character of love.
>
> **pre-1888 Adventism:** Replaced the "God is love/ with us" glasses with the law of God. Thus, they

reinterpreted Adventism's complete system of truth through the lens of the law and end time events. Jesus and his sanctuary were reinterpreted via the new law-glasses.

Historic Adventism: Took over where pre-1888 Adventism left off. Replaced the "God is love/ with us" glasses with character perfection. Thus, they reinterpreted Adventism's complete system of truth through the lens of perfectionism and end time events.

Reactionary Adventism: Reacted to the decades of legalism by rejecting the law-centred/ perfectionistic presuppositions. Made the assurance of salvation the new "glasses" used to read the Bible and consequently downplayed (and at times rejects entirely) Adventism's complete system of truth derived from its sanctuary focus.

Where we are Today

In the midst of all of these developments it is clear that what has been lost is the sanctuary narrative that gave Adventism a complete system of truth centred on Jesus. Those who continue to promote what they refer to as Historic, conservative Adventism view the entire narrative of scripture through the glasses of character perfection and the law. Those who promote a gospel-centred brand tend to be so reactionary to the conservatives that they down play anything that is not "salvational". Instead, they see the entire story through the presupposition of assurance of salvation. For them, so long as this is understood nothing else really matters. What both camps fail to realize is that they are both using man-centred glasses to interpret the story of scripture whereas the early Adventist sanctuary presupposition held that it was God's character of love, and not mankind, that was the central interpretive theme. And in both cases the sanctuary-God of early Adventism that provided the church with the holistic picture of God's love unheard of in Christian history has been forgotten. The conservatives continue to promote a rigid and legal view of God whereas the reactionaries continue to promote the same "incomplete" narrative of God's love found in other denominations. Add to this fundamental issue the myriad of other theological and cultural challenges that the church is currently divided over and you end up disoriented. And this is the context in which the church currently finds itself.

Conclusion

So if Adventism is, at its essence, the most complete understanding of the love of God in the Christian world, why is it so "non-loving" to so many people? Why have our preachers tended to emphasize a scary picture of judgment, perfectionistic ideologies and - quite frankly - legalistic and man-centred theology? Why are so many of our churches cold and dead?"

The answer can be narrowed down to this: *we have forgotten our story.*

The legalism that took over has resulted in a sectarian and narcissistic culture of elitism and holier-than-thou personalities. The beauty of Adventism has been adulterated by a foreign world-view that has, in many ways, "cast down the sanctuary". That "God with us" narrative has been morphed into a "God against us" theology comparable only to the errors of the medieval church. The trail of broken spirits, wounded sojourners and demoralized seekers that follows us cannot be excused in any way.

In reaction, others have come to the defence of Adventism by replacing perfectionism as a set of glasses with assurance and while they have succeeded at restoring the assurance of salvation lost in the eras of legalism, they have unwittingly assumed that themes like the law, prophecy, end time events etc. are staples of an old and worn out legacy of legalism. The result has been a new generation of Adventists more concerned with their personal assurance than with the character of God as revealed in every theme of scripture. Thus the health message, prophetic gift and end times narratives are either ignored, rejected or unknown. In all of this, the unique position of Adventism as a holistic God-is-love narrative unheard of anywhere in the Christian world remains in the background.

Group Questions

1. Have you been exposed to any of the ideas explored in this chapter? How have they impacted you or people you know in the church?
2. How do you feel about the historical tendency in Adventism to replace the sanctuary lens with man-centred ideas?
3. Is it clearer, after exploring the history, how a movement based on the love of God could lose its way?
4. What does this history say to us about the importance of keeping Jesus at the centre?
5. How can you begin bringing Jesus back into the centre of your experience and the life of your church?

CHAPTER 5: A WEIRDVOLUTION

So what can Adventism do to correct its course? Is it possible for us to create a culture that is in harmony with our narrative; centred in Jesus and expressing the totality of God's love?

I believe so. However, the solution I would like to propose as we close has nothing to do with church administration. Rather, I would like to focus on the grass roots - that is you and me. And here is my solution: We, as every day Seventh-day Adventist church members need to launch a "Weirdvolution or Weirdformation" aimed at remembering our story, building upon it and communicating it.

Allow me a few more moments to expand on each of these.

Remember our Story

Remembering our story begins with the question, What is our story? This question was answered in the previous chapter. But to summarize, it's really very simple. Adventism's story begins with two foundations. The first is that God is other-centred love at its purest. The second is that his entire redemptive plan takes place in harmony with human time. The first reveals the essence of his character. The second applies that essence to all his dealings with men. And the end result is a narrative that is not only Christ-centred, but Christ-filled.

To put it differently, Jesus is not only the centre of scripture, he is its fullness. Thus, Adventism is a story that is not about Adventism. Rather, it is a story about the character of God. Through this "God-is-love/ with us" lens, we understand every other theme of the Bible including the law, end time events, spiritual gifts, the judgment, the state of the dead and the fate of the wicked.

Ellen White spoke of the importance of the sanctuary when she wrote that our minds should "be directed to the heavenly sanctuary"[1] for the foundation of our faith is found in "[t]he correct understanding of the ministration in the heavenly sanctuary".[2] But Ellen White was not alone. "The pioneers of the movement saw the sanctuary truth as basic to the whole structure of Seventh-day Adventist doctrine."[3] Thus, James White could say that, "The subject of the sanctuary should be carefully examined, as it lies at the foundation of our faith and hope."[4] In the sanctuary, Adventism finds a "harmonious exposition of the Scriptures"[5] that is unheard of in the Christian world. It is "the truth that has made us what we are"[6] and the "foundation for our faith."[7]

In Exodus 25:8 God instructs the nation of Israel to make him a sanctuary so that he could "dwell among them". In contrast to the pagan gods who wanted little to do with their worshipers, the God of Israel desired to "dwell among the sons of Israel and... be their God" (Exodus 29:45).

While the theme of the sanctuary is deep and broad its simplest meaning is that it communicates God's desire to be with us, in our time and space, in intimate relationship. Thus, the sanctuary reveals God's closeness to us and his desire to be with us. His redemptive plan is ministered on our behalf there (Hebrews 8:2) and through it we come to understand his character of love, his plan of salvation and his eventual triumph over sin. Of the sanctuary David said, it reveals Gods "power and glory" (Psalm 63:2) and the narrative of justice and redemption (Psalm 73:17). This theme permeates the entire arch of scripture, which ends with the promise, "'Behold, the dwelling place of God is with man, and He will live with them. They will be His people, and God Himself will be with them as their God'" (Revelation 21:3)

Some may ask, "Don't all Christians believe that God is with us?" And the answer is yes. But the difference is that in Adventism, God's "withness" is not simply a belief, *it is a means by which we interpret every theme of scripture.*

For Adventism then, the entire Bible is to be understood, not through the lens of perfection, assurance, culture, philosophy or some other pet doctrine but through the lens of a God who loves relentlessly and desires, from his high and lofty throne, to be with us. This "interpretive lens", combined with our commitment to the centrality of Jesus, gives us a fresh approach to the law, the Sabbath, the covenants, the angelic realm, the rebellion of Satan, the judgment of God, the prophetic timeline, the treatment of our bodies, the gospel, justification and sanctification, end time events and the process of judgment.

As was made clear, it is not necessarily what we believe about each of these doctrines that is unique, for our beliefs are shared interdenominationally. Rather, it is the way in which the sanctuary has strung them together into a rhythm that reveals God's character through and through. And the tragedy of Adventism is that we continue to redefine our narrative with man-centred concepts. We continue to turn the story of God into the story of us. My assurance. My character perfection. My culture. My pet doctrine. My favourite philosophy. And we have forgotten that it's not about us. The Great Controversy is over the character of God. Who is he? What is he like? And how does every theme of scripture from law to grace, from Israel to church, from the former things of old to the things that are yet to come, reveal the truth about God's love?

The clearest evidence of how far we have fallen from our identity is seen in nearly every local church. If you are a pastor perhaps you have been repeatedly exposed to church members who complain that we focus too much on God's love and don't preach the distinctives anymore. These criticisms are frustrating to those of us who know that the only thing worth talking about is the love of God. However, the complaints may not necessarily come from a bad place. Instead, many are rightly annoyed by the rising trend to focus on the same surface message found in other Arminian denominations that speak of God's love all the time but cannot provide any deep and meaningful exposition of scriptures narrative. The sad part though is many of our members think the only alternative is to preach the distinctives while downplaying the love and grace of God. They have no idea that Adventism – as the only full story approach to the love of God – is itself the alternative. It celebrates the centrality and supremacy of Jesus and the revelation of God's character of love through all of scripture.

Think of it this way. Imagine a table full of microscopes all different colours, sizes and zoom capacities. Now Imagine one glass base that all of those microscopes took turns looking at. Each of the microscopes would provide a different view of the contents on that glass base. As you looked through each of them you would see more or different details than the other microscope can offer and it is amazing!

Now imagine someone walks in and rather than looking through the microscopes at the contents on the glass, they marvel at the microscopes instead and never look through them. How weird would that be?

And yet, that's exactly what Adventists do. That glass base is the love of God. The microscopes are doctrine. Each doctrine reveals different details and angles on the love of God. They are meant to be looked through, not merely looked at. And yet, how many of us obsess over the doctrines by looking at them, but never resolve to look through them?

That is the uniqueness of Adventism. It is about nothing other than the love of God as found in the person of Jesus and every doctrine it presents we explore gladly because we know that as we look through it, we will discover more about the unfailing love of God.

Build upon our Story

Once we have remembered our story, we need to build upon it. And at this point I need to make a huge clarification. This current book may give the impression that there was a "golden age" of Adventism. A time in which we had it all together but this is not the case. Adventism has never had a golden era. But what our pioneers had was a clear vision of how scripture was to be understood. From there they began to put the pieces together and develop the holistic system of truth we call Adventism.

But they only got so far before the church veered off into legalism and every other distraction that has gotten in the way since. To this day, the whole Bible approach to the love of God that Adventism is has yet to be fully realised. As I write, we are once again inundated with distractions and divisions over church authority and ordination and these themes are diverging us from realising who we are and what we have been called to say. I am not saying that our present debates are useless for they are very relevant. But we cannot allow them to take us away from developing our theological narrative. We put that task on the back burner for far too long. The foundation for a beautiful theological narrative is there and from it we can build toward a greater understanding of God's love and take the church and the culture by storm.

And it's not like we have a choice. We are told that "[t]he last rays of merciful light, the last message of mercy to be given to the world, is a revelation of His character of love."[8] And it is through the "God is love/with us" approach to unravelling the mysteries of scripture that this can become a reality.

Communicate our Story

Rediscovering Adventism should awaken a new generation to the beauty and relevance of what we have to say. And from there, every ounce of Adventist talent needs to be released. Musicians, artists, poets, writers, bloggers, designers, videographers, educators etc. But they cannot be stifled by conservative cultural expectations. Rather, they need to be set free with creative control - directed by the holistic narrative of Adventism - to plant new churches with new cultures, write new songs and create films, vlogs, art and other relevant resources that communicate our story in culturally savvy ways.[9]

Adventism, especially western Adventism, needs to stop pretending that one has to be a good European first before you can be a good Adventist. We need to stop conflating holiness with Eurocentrism. You don't have to look like, sound like, dress like or act like a cultured European to be holy. And it is that false notion (reflected in ideas like "Hymns-only", "KJV-only", "suit-and-tie-only" and the notion that classical music is inherently more sacred than music from tribal cultures) that stifles our young people's creativity.

European/ Victorian Adventism may be a beautiful expression of faith in its own right, but to act as though any deviation from this man made cultural mode is sinful is idolatry at best. To criticise the worship expression of diverse cultures and generations just because it doesn't look or sound like 1950's Caucasian Adventism is to place man made value structures equal to the word of God. News flash, God is not old and he is not a middle class

American from the 1950's. Holiness and European worship, dress and life styles are not the same thing.

We also need to get over this idea that new equals dangerous. For some reason, Adventist culture has developed this idea that if its new, if it's different or if its innovative then we are opening the door to deception. H.M.S. Richards faced strong criticism as he pioneered radio evangelism. "The radio is of the devil!" His critics shouted. Likewise, TV evangelism and now, digital/ social media evangelism is facing the same criticisms. In 2015, an innovative mini-film adaptation of the Great Controversy known as "The Record Keeper" was protested and eventually shut down because it didn't appeal to the old guard mentality. And in local churches everywhere, any attempt to try something new is always met with resistance and suspicion.

Ellen White cautioned against this sort of mentality and strongly advocated for innovative ministry. In Evangelism page 70 she writes, "New methods must be introduced. God's people must awake to the necessities of the time in which they are living. God has men whom He will call into His service,—men who will not carry forward the work in the lifeless way in which it has been carried forward in the past...."

This posture advocating for innovation and creativity is repeated constantly in her counsels (see Appendix A) and is one that local church leaders need to embrace and promote with passion.

We need to live, once more, as movement eager for the return of Jesus. We need to live once more as people aware of the prophetic events that have been foretold and be unashamed to speak hope into our communities. Our church services need to celebrate our holistic story as well. New songs need to be written for us to worship with - songs that capture the beauty of our holistic narrative. New churches need to be planted with new structures and architecture based on the foundation of this God of love and withness. We need to create ministries and projects designed for the salvation of the lost, not the comfort of the saint. We need new Bible study resources that teach the narrative of Adventism - not just disjointed doctrines. We need a deeper commitment to social service and justice from a "sanctuary perspective".

We need to reject any tradition and custom that gets in the way of connecting with a broken culture and preparing it for the judgment currently taking place. We need a unity based on the sanctuary God - a unity that is built on the knowledge that God is working in all cultures, at all times and in diverse manners. Such a worldview would provide a strong foundation to unity in diversity as opposed to the relativism that is often used. And most importantly, we need to be a sanctuary people by becoming centres of influence - "little sanctuaries" that reflect God's love and desire to be with us by coming close to our communities and being "with" them in intimate ways.

If we take our beliefs serious we can't get away from the fact that the sanctuary vision "call[s] us to step out of our spiritual myopia and become actively involved in helping the addicted, the broken, the lonely. It is a call to reach out to this lost world with more urgency than ever before that they may come to know Christ and his cleansing blood..."[10]

But how? Any reasonable person will see a gargantuan checklist in this chapter – things I believe need to change in our church. And that's only the start! So how can we accomplish this without being overwhelmed? I think the answer lies at the heart of our story: Jesus. If we simply focus on making Jesus the centre of our faith and remove anything from the centre that doesn't belong there I believe the things expressed in this chapter, plus many others, will simply fall into place all on their own. Jesus is the answer and as we turn our eyes to him, seeking to define our faith and practice in his person and by his grace, we will experience a metamorphosis in our churches. This change will be actuated and maintained, not by human methods or strategies, but by the Spirit of our God.

Conclusion

I do not pretend to have all the answers. Neither do I pretend that a renewed "God is love/ with us" presupposition would magically solve all of the problems in the church. But one thing I am convinced of - we have to remember our story. Because our story is not about us. It's about him. And until we choose, from the ground up, to rediscover the narrative of Adventism as a narrative about God's character of love we will continue to wander aimlessly amidst a broken, post-church culture seeking answers to questions that God has already given us. We will continue to perpetuate dead and vision-less churches that "major in the minors" and have little to no connection with the communities in which they reside.

Although the sanctuary narrative is inexhaustible, I love how Ellen White summarized it in the following statement.

> In the temple in heaven, the dwelling place of God, His throne is established in righteousness and judgment. In the most holy place is His law, the great rule of right by which all mankind are tested. The ark that enshrines the tables of the law is covered with the mercy seat, before which Christ pleads His blood in the sinner's behalf. Thus is represented the union of justice and mercy in the plan of human redemption. This union infinite wisdom alone could devise and infinite power accomplish; it is a union that fills all heaven with

> wonder and adoration. The cherubim of the earthly sanctuary, looking reverently down upon the mercy seat, represent the interest with which the heavenly host contemplate the work of redemption. This is the mystery of mercy into which angels desire to look—that God can be just while He justifies the repenting sinner and renews His intercourse with the fallen race; that Christ could stoop to raise unnumbered multitudes from the abyss of ruin and clothe them with the spotless garments of His own righteousness to unite with angels who have never fallen and to dwell forever in the presence of God.[11]

Notice that in this statement is found nearly every theme in scripture. In it we find God's character of love and desire to be with us. We find his holiness, his power and his wisdom. We find his justice. His law, judgment and mercy are also there. Jesus as our mediator, his blood and our redemption are central. Heaven is there. Angels are there. The battle between good and evil is there and toward the end we are once again reminded of God's intimacy with us, Christs salvific power and grace and love and - at last - the ultimate end of the narrative of scripture: our eternal reunion with our creator for which he gave his son on the cross.

This whole-Bible approach to the love of God is what Adventism is all about. He is a sanctuary God - a God of "withness" - who both loves us and longs to be with us. That is our story and we tell it, not only in one or two books in the Bible, not only with a side blinded focus on the law, assurance or any other doctrine, but in every theme and song and prophecy.

And we must do so, until the day finally arrives when "[o]ne pulse of harmony and gladness beats through the vast creation. From Him who created all, flow life and light and gladness, throughout the realms of illimitable space. From the minutest atom to the greatest world, all things, animate and inanimate, in their unshadowed beauty and perfect joy, declare that God is love."[12]

Group Questions

1. What steps can you take today to lead your local church to remember its story? (ex. Preach a sermon series, start a small group going through this book, discover it for myself and share it with others).
2. What steps can you take to build on our story and discover more of God's love in scripture?
3. What steps can you take to create a culture of innovation and creativity in your local church?
4. How do you feel about the invitation to launch a "Weirdvolution" in your local church? Share your thoughts and emotions with the group and be as honest as possible.

CHAPTER 6: A WEIRD CONCLUSION

Why is the local SDA church dead? In this book, I have offered the single reason why our churches are struggling. It has more to do with not knowing why we are here and less to do with our strategies and methods.

About a month ago the local pastors where I work gathered for a series of lectures by a retired Adventist professor from Yorkshire. I can't remember his name, but I do remember a story he told. He had met with a novelist at a local café and she asked him why he was an Adventist. Rather than give her some theological answer he explained to her what Adventism meant to him and framed the discussion in terms of the Sabbath. His answer had nothing to do with the perpetuity of the law or religious arguments. Rather, it was about God's love impacting his life in time and space, and bringing meaning and value to his existence.

When he finished, the woman who was not a Christian at all replied, "How frightfully inspiring."

If you asked your church members why they are Adventist would anything they said be "frightfully inspiring?" In my experience the answer is a clear *no.* More often than not, what we have to say is monotonous and meaningless. This is a symptom of a people who have lost sight of their story as it is in Jesus - and that is our real problem.

Think about it. How many Adventists think our mission is to tell the world about the Mark of the Beast? Haven't you heard those members who complain that we don't preach enough sermons about the Pope and end time events? And then there are the ones on the other end of the spectrum who are so fed up with the unhealthy attitudes that they would rather never hear another sermon on end times again.

The real issue here is a culture with no story. And if we don't have a story then what do we have? And here is my point. You can focus on small groups, mission and service projects and discipleship pathways all you want. Until you rediscover, as a church, why you exist you will never come alive. You might gain some traction and activity, but you won't have the passion to turn the world upside down.

Imagine with me a local church that gets it. Imagine a congregation full of people who understand that Adventism is literally the only whole Bible approach to the love of God. How passionate would they be knowing that they hold a scarce treasure that seekers can find nowhere else? Will those people be satisfied with no outreach? Will they be okay with stagnating and dragging their feet for the next ten years? Or will they long to spread, plant churches and shout the story loud?

In other words, what we need are weird people in love with this weird story who do weird things just to tell the next person about this weird God of love who defies all our expectations. You can't be a traditionalist and be weird. Traditionalists are too predictable. You can't be conservative and be weird. Conservatives are too cautious. You can't be a compromiser and be weird. Compromisers are too spineless. You can't be like everyone else and be weird. Being like everyone else is too ordinary. Our weirdness calls us to be counter-cultural, eccentric and redemptively bizarre. It calls us to radical innovation and wild imagination. We have something weird to say that no one else is saying – so let's start talking!

My encouragement to you, as a reader, is this. Don't just read this book. Share it. Preach it. Tell it. Get a group at your church to read it together. Got through the group questions at the end of each chapter. Let that small group get excited. Let them see why we exist. Then get them to spread it. Let's awaken our sense of purpose again. Let every person in that church know exactly why we are here. We are here to tell a weird story of a God of indescribable love that no one else is telling.

This book is not designed to be the end of the conversation. It's here to get it started. It merely introduces the topic. It offers a starting place for rediscovering why we are here and allowing that story to redefine everything we do as a local church.

In the future I will release "Story Church", a second book that will go into more practical, local church steps you can take to redesign your local Adventist church for mission. But in the meantime, do some ground work by redesigning the way your members and leaders think. May your goal be for every person in that room to know why their church exists. May their answer be: *To tell the world the most compelling story of God's love they have ever heard.*

How frightfully inspiring.

APPENDIX A

I once read a book that lamented the good ol' days when Christians rejected anything that was new. As you can imagine, the book was anti-new. This is a common view held in every denomination by what many have dubbed the traditionalists. Traditionalists are known by their fear, dislike, or suspicion of anything and everything that is new. In one sense, their fears are well founded. Jude wrote:

> Beloved, while I was very diligent to write to you concerning our common salvation, I found it necessary to write to you exhorting you to contend earnestly for the faith which was once for all delivered to the saints. - Jude 1:3

For Jude, it was "the faith which was once for all delivered to the saints" that was the true faith. Anything new was to be discarded. In the same way, modern attempts to reinterpret Genesis 1 - 11 as allegorical, merge Christianity with other religions, or undermine the central pillars of biblical Christianity should be rejected.*

However, not everything that is new is bad. It was in the name of "the old ways" that many of the Pharisees refused to come to Jesus or accept Christianity. Likewise, 1888 taught the Adventist church the danger of rejecting new light simply because it is new. Many in those years patronized themselves and one another with "sticking to the old ways." Such an attitude made many feel as though they were standing for the truth though the heavens fall. But the reality was that they rejected the Holy Spirit who was trying to bring them to a new experience and traded Gods will for their lives for their allegiance to "the old ways."

However, history shows that the Adventist church is riddled with the new. A new understanding of the Sabbath, a new view of the state of the dead and hell, a new revelation of the sanctuary doctrine, a new emphasis on health and education. We were on the cutting edge with sanitariums and Christian education, have a new prophet, a new style of evangelism, and a new message. Adventism, it seems, was all about the new. In keeping with the flow Ellen White made the following comments on outreach, evangelism, and the need of the new:

In the cities of today, where there is so much to attract and please, the people can be interested by no ordinary efforts.... put forth extraordinary efforts in order to arrest the attention of the multitudes.... make use of every means that can possibly be devised for causing the truth to stand out clearly and distinctly. {Ev 40.3}

The methods and means by which we reach certain ends are not always the same. The missionary must use reason and judgment. Changes for the better must be made... {GW 468.3}

Let us not forget that different methods are to be employed to save different ones. {Ev 106.2}

Different methods of labor are really essential in sowing the seeds of truth and gathering in the harvest. {TM 251.1}

New methods must be introduced. God's people must awake to the necessities of the time in which they are living. God has men whom He will call into His service,—men who will not carry forward the work in the lifeless way in which it has been carried forward in the past.... {Ev 70.1}

Whatever may have been your former practice, it is not necessary to repeat it again and again in the same way. God would have new and untried methods followed. Break in upon the people—surprise them. {Ev 125.4}

Let every worker in the Master's vineyard, study, plan, devise methods, to reach the people where they are. We must do something out of the common course of things. We must arrest the attention. {Ev 122.4}

As field after field is entered, new methods and new plans will spring from new circumstances. New thoughts will come with the new workers who give themselves to the work. As they seek the Lord for help, He will communicate with them. They will receive plans devised by the Lord Himself. {6T 476.2}

We fully believe in church organization; but this is not to prescribe the exact way in which we should work, for not all minds are to be reached by the same methods. {6T 116.1}

There must be no fixed rules; our work is a progressive work, and there must be room left for methods to be improved upon. {Ev 105.1}

Some of the methods used in this work will be different from the methods used in the work in the past; but let no one, because of this, block the way by criticism. {Ev 105.2}

There is to be no unkind criticism, no pulling to pieces of another's work... {AA 275.2}

The leaders among God's people are to guard against the danger of condemning the methods of individual workers who are led by the Lord to do a special work that but few are

> fitted to do. Let brethren in responsibility be slow to criticize movements that are not in perfect harmony with their methods of labor. Let them never suppose that every plan should reflect their own personality. {9T 259}

With history, the insights of Ellen White, and the need of the hour I propose that it is time we stopped giving innovation the cold shoulder. We should not be so naive as to embrace every new thing but neither should we flip the "auto-pilot of rejection to anything new" switch. We need new. We need innovation. If we embrace this reality and seek God for those new ideas and methods of evangelism and outreach the results, I'm sure, will be stunning.

---

* While any new anti-biblical teachings should be rejected we must always do so intelligently and graciously not dogmatically. Behind every teaching is a soul for whom Christ died and they must never be mistreated for their faith regardless of how much it differs from our own.

Thanks to Russel Burril's How to Grow an Adventist Church for the compilation of Ellen White quotes.

This Appendix was originally published as "Was Ellen White Against Anything New?" at: https://thestorychurchproject.com/bloghost//2013/11/was-ellen-white-against-anything-new.html

APPENDIX B

Years ago I had the opportunity to preach my first, entire evangelistic series. The series was called "Revelations Hope" and I, along with the other students, was given an entire set of presentations to use as my sermons. The idea was, as it has always been, to present the unique Adventist doctrines (known as "present truth") to those who had never heard them before. Being a lover of present truth one would easily guess I enjoyed the experience. But I didn't.

OK, let me be fair. I didn't hate the experience. However, I found it very difficult to enjoy. There was just too much weird stuff going on. First of all, the series was marketed as "Revelations Hope" and gave the impression that it was going to be a seminar on the book of Revelation to help people understand this often confusing book. However, the series was more about Adventist doctrine than it was about Revelation and sadly enough, it used the book of Revelation sort of like a proof platform to launch into various topics that weren't in Revelation at all. But that isn't the part that really bothered me. What bothered me was that the series as a whole lacked the one thing it was meant to be proclaiming: "present truth."

Night after night I found myself editing the sermons that had been given to us. There was no way I was going to preach that stuff. It was overcomplicated. It was confusing. And worst of all, it lacked truth. Sure, the Sabbath was presented along with Daniel 2, the Investigative Judgment, the State of the Dead, etc. But I learned a long time ago that there is a difference between preaching present-facts and present-truth. As Adventists, we have historically prided ourselves in always having the right answers, but the world doesn't need right answers, it needs truth and there is a difference between the two.

It wasn't easy. At times I felt like a rebel. At times I felt arrogant. And at times I felt as though I was somehow in the wrong. *Maybe the way it's always been done is the right way*, I thought. *Maybe I am diluting the message by making them so simple and Christ-centred.* And so on and so forth. But I pressed on because the truth is, I just couldn't preach those sermons. They were full of "answers" and "facts" but they didn't have truth - they didn't have Jesus. And anytime we preach present truth without Jesus we engage in one of Satan's master deceptions - the dissolution of present truth.

The deception is powerful for this reason: By preaching doctrine void of Christ many Adventists think they are actually preaching Christ. In other words, none of these Christless sermons are ever even perceived to be Christless. Most Adventists never see anything wrong with them and if asked, many would say that the sermons are indeed Christ-centred. But allow me to set the record straight: Mentioning Jesus at the end of your sermon, quoting his words, or having Power Point slides with his pictures don't actually make a sermon Christ-centred. A sermon is Christ-centred when the entire thesis is drenched in the blood of Jesus. A sermon is Christ-centred when, no matter your topic, Jesus is presented in all of his beauty and majesty. A sermon is Christ-centred when it results in repentance, faith, and a greater love for God. A sermon is Christ-centred when it inspires change as opposed to requiring it. A sermon is Christ-centred when it reveals Jesus' more and not simply some biblical concept that other churches aren't teaching. A sermon is Christ-centred when both preacher and listener leave the church and they know, they just know, that they have been with Jesus.

You can preach doctrine and theology all you want. You can have the right answers and the right facts, but that doesn't make it truth. Truth is discovered only when it is found in Jesus. "The seventh day is the Sabbath" is not truth. It is a biblical fact. Jesus said, "I am the...truth" and any sermon that lifts up doctrine without lifting up Jesus does not deserve to be called present truth. Call it present facts or present answers, or present points or present information, but don't call it present truth.

> The sacrifice of Christ as an atonement for sin is the great truth around which all other truths cluster. In order to be rightly understood and appreciated, every truth in the Word of God, from Genesis to Revelation, must be studied in the light that streams from the cross of Calvary. I present before you the great, grand monument of mercy and regeneration, salvation and redemption–the Son of God uplifted on the cross. This is to be the foundation of every

discourse given by our ministers.—Gospel Workers, 315 (1915).

This Appendix was originally published as "The Cross & The Dissolution Of Present Truth" at: https://thestorychurchproject.com/bloghost//2014/08/the-cross-dissolution-of-present-truth.html

Chapter End Notes

Chapter 2

[1] Miller, Nicholas P. "The Reformation and the Remnant", Accesed via Kindle, (location 2106-07).
[2] http://www.christianity.com/church/church-history/the-five-solas-of-the-protestant-reformation.html
[3] https://en.wikipedia.org/wiki/Arminianism
[4] http://evangelicalarminians.org/john-wesley-on-the-origins-of-evil/
[5] http://evangelicalarminians.org/demarcating-wesleyan-arminianism-and-reformed-arminianism/
[6] The doctrine of perfection in Wesleyan and Adventist theology is not to be confused with the heresy of sinless perfectionism. One is rooted in the concept of perfection in love as an aim of the sanctification journey whereas the other is rooted in semi-pelagian ideologies and place the attainment of this perfection as the true foundation for justification. For more on Wesley's doctrine of perfection see: https://www.olivetree.com/store/product.php?productid=17158
[7] While Adventists believe in the 7th day Sabbath as opposed to a Sunday Sabbath the foundations for our teaching are actually identical to those espoused by these historic protestant positions. And even this is not unique. Our belief in the 7th day Sabbath came to us from the Seventh Day Baptists. For more on the 2nd London Baptist confession visit: http://www.1689federalism.com/
[8] Knight, George R. "A Search For Identity" Accessed via Google Books, (pg 19).
[9] http://www.sealingtime.com/resources/online-

library/books/other/thomas-tillam/the-seventh-day-sabbath-sought-out-thomas-tillam-1657
[10] For more on Adventism and the covenants see: "The Hole in Adventism": https://thestorychurchproject.com/store
[11] http://rethinkinghell.com/
[12] Protestant Reformers had a major interest in historicism, with a direct application to their struggle against the Papacy. Prominent leaders and scholars among them, including Martin Luther, John Calvin, Thomas Cranmer, John Thomas, John Knox, and Cotton Mather, identified the Roman Papacy as the Antichrist. The Centuriators of Magdeburg, a group of Lutheran scholars in Magdeburg headed by Matthias Flacius, wrote the 12-volume "Magdeburg Centuries" to discredit the papacy and identify the pope as the Antichrist.
https://en.wikipedia.org/wiki/Historicism_(Christianity)#Protestant
[13] https://thestorychurchproject.com/bloghost//2012/10/the-pre-advent-judgment-5-ij-is-not.html?rq=investigative%20judgment
[14] https://en.wikipedia.org/wiki/Christian_mortalism#The_Reformation
[15] While Luther cannot be regarded as fully in agreement with standard soul-sleep theology he nevertheless was a protestant forerunner to it. For a thorough analysis see:
http://www.atsjats.org/publication_file.php?pub_id=398
[16]
[17] Miller, Nicholas P. "The Reformation and the Remnant", Accessed via Kindle, (location 2107-09).
[18]Weber, Martin. www.sdaforme.com
[19] Miller, Nicholas P. "The Reformation and the Remnant", Accessed via Kindle, (location 2116-19).
[20] Knight, George R. "Another Look at Babylon"

https://www.ministrymagazine.org/archive/2002/04/another-look-at-babylon.html
[21] Torres, Marcos D. "The One Project: Danger or Blessing?"
https://thestorychurchproject.com/bloghost//2014/08/the-one-project-danger-or-blessing.html

Chapter 3

Note: Certain portions of this chapter are edited excerpts of the series: "The Hole in Adventism: Identifying our Place in the Continuum of Protestant Covenantal Thought". The original source of these excerpts has not been cited in order to maximize reader experience. You can access that source here.

[1] http://proto-protestantism.blogspot.com.au/p/who-were-proto-protestants.html
[2] Bishop, Paul A., "Martin Luther and the Protestant Reformation":
https://www.hccfl.edu/media/173616/ee2luther.pdf
[3] https://www.calvinistcorner.com/tulip.htm
[4] http://evangelicalarminians.org/the-five-points-of-arminianism-calvinism/
[5] Appel, Dan. "7 Important Questions About 1844":
https://atoday.org/7-important-questions-about-1844/
[6] Manea, Mike C. & Marcos D Torres, "Why the Critics of the Investigative Judgment Have Failed":
https://thestorychurchproject.com/bloghost//2016/01/why-critics-of-investigative-judgment.html
[7] In other words, no doctrine of the church would have failed to develop if we did not have this date. Our judgment narrative would simply have different chronology. But the narrative itself would remain intact.

[8] Castro, Diane. "Presuppositions and Interpretations: How Our Assumptions Affect Our Understanding of the Bible, Part 1 of 3,": http://blogs.christianpost.com/ambassador-of-reconciliation/presuppositions-and-interpretations-how-our-assumptions-affect-our-understanding-of-the-bible-part-1-of-2-7212/

[9] Dongell, Joseph. "10 Things I Wish Everyone Knew About Arminianism
": https://www.onfaith.co/discussion/10-things-i-wish-everyone-knew-about-arminianism

[10] Canale, Fernando. "Toward a Criticism of Theological Reason : Time and Timelessness as Primordial Presuppositions" (1983). Dissertations. 22. See also, Roger E Olson. "An Example of Unwarranted Theological Speculation: Divine Timelessness,": http://www.patheos.com/blogs/rogereolson/2015/02/an-example-of-unwarranted-theological-speculation-divine-timelessness/
http://digitalcommons.andrews.edu/dissertations/22

[11] Not all Calvinists agree that God decreed who goes to hell. Arminians, on the other hand, argue that predestination is unjust and unloving in all of its forms. For more information on the different views in the Calvinist camp see:
https://www.gotquestions.org/lapsarianism.html

[12] Pedlar, James. "John Wesley on Predestination": https://jamespedlar.wordpress.com/2012/02/16/john-wesley-on-predestination/

[13] This does not mean that all Calvinists agree on all things. Covenantalism is divided into differing camps such as the Westminster Confession, the Asbury Declaration, and 1689 Federalism. However, the disagreements in these views are often minor. They all present a very unified approach to understanding the whole Bible through the Calvinist lens.

[14] For more on the history of the Middle Story see Miller, Nicholas. "God's Moral Government of Love: The Theology that Helped Shape the Movement for Abolition and Civil Rights,": https://law.pepperdine.edu/nootbaar-institute/annual-conference/loveandlaw/presentations/miller-paper.pdf
[15] For more on Wesley's "Aesthetic Theme" see: Bryant, Barry E. "John Wesley On the Origins of Evil,": http://evangelicalarminians.org/john-wesley-on-the-origins-of-evil/
[16] Dongell, Joseph. "10 Things I Wish Everyone Knew About Arminianism
": https://www.onfaith.co/discussion/10-things-i-wish-everyone-knew-about-arminianism
[17] see for example: http://evangelicalarminians.org/a-short-partially-annotated-list-of-arminian-systematic-theologies/
[18] ibid
[19] See for example: Markey, Dell. "Wesleyan Church vs. Methodist
Church,": http://classroom.synonym.com/wesleyan-church-vs-methodist-church-7572.html
[20] Challies, Tim. "Why I Am Not an Arminian,": https://www.challies.com/articles/why-i-am-not-arminian
[21] See Fudge, Edward. "Immortality is Conditional,": http://edwardfudge.com/2012/03/immortality-is-conditional/
[22] This does not mean that Adventism succeeded in this approach without much struggle. The history of Adventism shows that developing this "whole Bible" view of God's love took decades and, in fact, continues to this day. Throughout the years the church has had to confront numerous issues from false doctrines and teachers to administrative and ecclesiological challenges. All of this has slowed the process of the

stories development and, at times, distorted it requiring the church to backtrack, after the dust has settled, and continue its task. Therefore, this statement needs to be understood, not as a literal rendition of the development of Adventist thought, but as a summation of it historical trajectory and future potential. For more on the historical development of Adventist thought see: Knight, George R. "A Search for Identity: The Development of Seventh-Day Adventist Beliefs" and Miller, Nicholas. "The Reformation and the Remnant: The Reformers Speak to Today's Church"

[23] As mentioned earlier in the article, the timeless God foundation resulted in an incoherent system of thought for Arminians and is, quite possibly, the underlying reason why the movement never developed a cohesive "whole Bible" view. For more see: Blanco, Marcos. "Adventist Theology and the New Anthropology: Challenges and Opportunities": https://www.ministrymagazine.org/archive/2015/05/adventist-theology-and-the-new-anthropology
and, Canale, Fernando. "Toward a Criticism of Theological Reason : Time and Timelessness as Primordial Presuppositions" (1983). Dissertations. 22

[24] White, Ellen G. "Great Controversy," p. 488.

[25] White, Ellen G. "Christ Object Lessons," p. 415.

[26] White, Ellen G. "Evangelism," p. 22.

[27] Adrian Zahid summarized it well when he quoted various Adventist thinkers on the matter,
Canale suggests that, "The sanctuary doctrine is the most comprehensive doctrine or motif in Scripture and therefore plays a decisive role in guiding biblical interpretation and the construction of Adventist theology." James White saw that "the present truth is harmonious in all its parts; its links are all connected; the bearings of all its portions upon each other are like clockwork," LeRoy Froom wrote of early Adventist

theology as the "base of a coordinated system of truth." George Knight, writes that "Sabbatarian Adventists produced an integrated theology rather than a list of discrete doctrines, and Alberto Timm states that these beliefs were an integrated system related to the attributes of God." (Zahid, Adrian. "The One Project: The 'Jesus. All.' Paradox (Part 3)": https://thecompassmagazine.com/blog/the-one-project-the-jesus-all-paradox)

[28] For more on the Investigative Judgment as it relates to the Middle story and Gods moral government of love see: Torres, Marcos D. "The Pre-Advent Judgment": https://thestorychurchproject.com/search?q=pre-advent%20judgment

[29] For more on Historicism as understood through the love of God see Lightbearers series: "Covenant Kingdom" by David Asscherick, Fred Bischoff, James Rafferty, Jeffrey Rosario and Ty Gibson: http://www.lightbearers.org/resource/covenant-kingdom-01-the-covenant-lens/ For more on the necessity of Historicism over against other systems see, Manea, Mike. "Bible Prophecy for Atheists," (part 1-3): https://thecompassmagazine.com/author/mikemanea

[30] For more on Adventism and the doctrine of "remnant church" see: Torres, Marcos D. "The Remnant Church: Denominational Arrogance or Conviction?": https://thestorychurchproject.com/bloghost//2014/02/the-remnant-church-denominational.html

[31] In addition, the statement does not imply that the Seventh-day Adventist church is perfect from an administrative perspective. The church is still under the administration of erring mortals and as such, problems remain that slow - and at times - reverse the progress of building God's kingdom. This is to be expected in any organization.

[32] White, Ellen G. "Candid Investigation Necessary to an Understanding of the Truth,": https://m.egwwritings.org/en/book/820.10079

[33] At this juncture it is important for the reader to understand 3 points:

1) Adventism's "Sanctuary/ God-in-time" motif does not imply that God is somehow bound by time - a view held in Panentheistic and Pandeistic thought and which also forms a part of Open Theism/ Process theology. Adventism accepts the clear Biblical teaching that God is not bound by time and is completely separate from his creation (2 Pet. 3:8, Psa. 90:4, Isa. 57:15, John 4:24, Heb. 11:3). Rather, because the Bible never defines timelessness (what it looks like) Adventism refuses to use philosophical speculations about timelessness as a presupposition by which to interpret the Bible. Therefore, Adventism seeks to interpret scripture solely on what scripture reveals and this is a God who, while certainly separate from his creation (including time) voluntarily condescends into time and space in order to interact with his creation in intimacy. The sanctuary in scripture, which God commanded the Israelites to build so that he could "dwell among them" is also a revelation of the entire plan of salvation and was patterned after the sanctuary in heaven (Exodus 25:8-9; Hebrews 8:1-2, 5). This sanctuary in heaven thus reveals God's desire to "dwell among us" despite his transcendence and forms a Biblical interpretive framework for understanding the love and immanence of God in all of scripture. This love and immanence are revealed in the plan of salvation, the lamb slain from the foundation of the world (Jesus who is Emanuel - God with us), the high priestly ministry, the law, the judgment, etc.

2) Adventism is not alone in the "God-in-time" motif. Other Christian theologians and philosophers such as Roger E. Olson (Arminian), Richard Watson (Methodist),

I. A. Dorner (Lutheran-Reformed), Karl Barth (Reformed), John Polkinghorne (Anglican), and William L. Craig (Molinist) have also popularized and argued for this view (for more see: http://www.patheos.com/blogs/rogereolson/2015/02/an-example-of-unwarranted-theological-speculation-divine-timelessness/). Thus, even the God-in-time motif is not original to Adventism. What is original is that Adventism has pressed this view through the love of God and developed a way to understand scriptures themes through it - not via philosophy, but via scriptures internal "God-with-us" (sanctuary) hermeneutic.

3) It is also important for the reader to recognize that the sanctuary view in no way replaces the centrality of Jesus. Jesus is the centre of the sanctuary narrative. The sanctuary, rather than replacing the Jesus-only paradigm, reveals how the centrality of Jesus impacts every facet of the Big, Middle and Little story which in turn gives birth to a cohesive "whole-Bible" story of the love of God.

[34] White, Ellen G. "Christ Object Lessons," p. 415.

Chapter 4

Note: Certain portions of this chapter are edited excerpts of the article "REclaiming Adventism (A Response to the Testimony of former Adventist Eliana Matthews)". The original source of these excerpts has not been cited in order to maximize reader experience. You can access that source here.

[1] "Second Great Awakening": https://en.wikipedia.org/wiki/Second_Great_Awakening

[2] See Torres, Marcos D. "The Hole in Adventism: Identifying Our Place in the Continuum of Protestant

Covenantal Thought":
https://thestorychurchproject.com/store
[3] Weber, Timothy. "Dispensational Premillennialism: The Dispensationalist Era, How a once-mocked idea began its domination of the evangelical world":
http://www.christianitytoday.com/history/issues/issue-61/dispensational-premillennialism-dispensationalist-era.html
[4] Harbach, R. C. "Dispensationalism and the Christian Under Law":
http://www.reformedspokane.org/Doctrine_pages/The%20doctrine%20of%20the%20church/Church%20%26%20Israel/Dispensationalism_Harbach12.html
[5] see Knight, George R. "Ellen White's World: A Fascinating Look at the Times in which She Lived", (Ch 8: Religious Impulses).
[6] Nam, Julius. "Adventists in American Courts–The Sunday Law Cases":
http://spectrummagazine.org/article/julius-nam/2013/01/11/adventists-american-courts%E2%80%94-sunday-law-cases
[6] See Knight, George R. "A Search for Identity: The Development of Seventh-day Adventist Beliefs", (Ch 5: What is Christian in Adventism?).
[7] White, Ellen G. "Testimonies to Ministers", p. 92.
[8] Zahid, Adrian: "The One Project: The Jesus All Paradox (Part 3)":
https://thecompassmagazine.com/blog/the-one-project-the-jesus-all-paradox
[9] Knight, George R. "What Happened in 1888? A Historical Account of a Very Historic Event":
http://www.adventistreview.org/2013-1528-p16
[10] See Moore, A. Leroy. "Adventist Cultures in Conflict: Principles of Reconciliation"
[11] White, Ellen G. "The Review and Herald", (March 11, 1890).

[12] White, Ellen G. "The Review and Herald", (April 1, 1890).
[13] Knight, George R. "What Happened in 1888? A Historical Account of a Very Historic Event": http://www.adventistreview.org/2013-1528-p16
[14] Maxwell, C. Mervyn. "What is the 1888 Message?": https://www.ministrymagazine.org/archive/1988/02/what-is-the-1888-message
[15] White, Ellen G. "Faith and Works" p. 25.
[16] White, Ellen G. "The Review and Herald Extra", (December 23, 1890). Notice the question, "Is the lamp of God's love to go out in darkness?" This "lamp" Ellen White speaks of is the Adventist movement, which as we saw in the previous chapter, stands alone in the Christian world in terms of its whole-Bible approach to the love of God. When the gospel was rejected by many church members and leaders, Ellen White mourned the possibility that without Jesus as the unifying element of all of scripture, Adventism's lamp which shone brightly on the love of God would go out in darkness. Such a context sheds light on her renewed emphasis on Jesus following 1888 where she authored classic works such as "The Desire of Ages" (a commentary on the four gospels) and her signature book "Steps to Christ".
[17] See Timm, Alberto R. "A History of Seventh-day Adventist Views on Biblical and Prophetic Inspiration", (1844-2000): [http://www.academia.edu/7797182/A_History_of_Seventh-day_Adventist_Views_on_Biblical_and_Prophetic_Inspiration_1844%C3%902000]; and Knight, George R. "A Search for Identity: The Development of Seventh-day Adventist Beliefs", (Ch 6 What is Fundamentalist in Adventism?)
[18] Zahid, Adrian: "The One Project: The Jesus All Paradox (Part 3)":

https://thecompassmagazine.com/blog/the-one-project-the-jesus-all-paradox
[19] Canale, Fernando. "The Eclipse of Scripture and the Protestantization of the Adventist Mind: Part 1: The Assumed Compatibility of Adventism with Evangelical Theology and Ministerial Practices" p. 137, footnote 11, [http://www.atsjats.org/publication_file.php?pub_id=374&journal=1&type=pdf]
[20] See Hayden, Kevin. "Lifestyles of the Remnant: A Refreshing Look at the Principles of Christian Living" and Weber, Martin. "Adventist Hot Potatoes".
[21] See Knight, George R. "Myths in Adventism"
[22] See Moore, A. Leroy. "Questions on Doctrine Revisited?"
[23] See Torres, Marcos D. "Reclaiming Adventism": https://thestorychurchproject.com/bloghost//2013/08/reclaiming-adventism-response-to.html
[24] ibid.
[25] Zahid, Adrian: "The One Project: The Jesus All Paradox (Part 3)":
https://thecompassmagazine.com/blog/the-one-project-the-jesus-all-paradox
[26] Manea, Mike. Biblical VS Andreasenist LGT": http://mikemanea.com/conversations/biblical-vs-andreasenist-lgt/
[27] Johns, W.H. "The ABCs of Dr. Desmond Ford's Theology":
https://www.adventistbiblicalresearch.org/sites/default/files/pdf/desmondfordtheology_0.pdf
[28] Nash, Andy. "Beyond Belief":
http://archives.adventistreview.org/article/6144/archives/issue-2013-1508/beyond-belief Andy Nash Beyond Belief
[29] See both "Seventh-day Adventist Young Adult Study," Barna Group, 2013:
http://www.youngadultlife.com/wp-

content/uploads/2015/01/Barna-SDA-Millennials-Report-final.pdf
and "21st Century Seventh-day Adventist Connection Study": https://www.adventistarchives.org/the-twenty-%C2%AD%E2%80%90first-century-seventh-%C2%AD%E2%80%90day-adventist-connection-study.pdf

Chapter 5

[1] White, Ellen G. "Selected Messages", p. 67.
[2] White, Ellen G. "Evangelism", p. 221.
[3] White, Ellen G. "Christ in His Sanctuary", p. 8.
[4] ibid.
[5] White, Ellen G. "The Great Controversy", p. 435.
[6] White, Ellen G. "Christ in His Sanctuary", p. 13.
[7] ibid. p. 12.
[8] White, Ellen G. "Christ Object Lessons", p. 415.
[9] See Asscherick, David. "The Ecclesiastical Trajectory of Reform": http://www.lightbearers.org/resource/session-15-the-ecclesiastical-trajectory-of-reform/
[10] Torres, Marcos D. "Adventism Oozes Social Justice, Do You?": https://thestorychurchproject.com/bloghost//2016/09/adventism-oozes-social-justice-do-you.html
[11] White, Ellen G. "Christ in His Sanctuary", p. 92.
[12] White, Ellen G. "The Great Controversy", p. 678.

marcos torres
THE HOLE IN ADVENTISM
Making Total Sense of the Old & New Covenant

Website

www.thestorychurchproject.com

Facebook, Twitter and Instagram

www.facebook.com/thestorychurchproject

www.twitter.com/storychurchproj

www.instagram.com/thestorychurchproject

www.ingramcontent.com/pod-product-compliance
Lightning Source LLC
Chambersburg PA
CBHW060801050426
42449CB00008B/1485

9780648565284